THE BRITISH LIBRARY
HISTORIC LIVES

The Duke of Wellington

THE BRITISH LIBRARY
HISTORIC LIVES

The Duke of
Wellington

Matthew Shaw

Cover illustration: *The Duke of Wellington* by Francisco Goya. *National Gallery, London*

Half-title page illustration: A daguerreotype of Wellington from 1844, when he was seventy-five years old. *Stratfield Saye. By permission of the trustees of the Duke of Wellington*

Title-page illustration: Funeral roll, showing the 33rd Regiment – The Duke's Own. *The British Library, HS 74/1739*

First published in 2005 by The British Library 96 Euston Road London NW1 2DB

Text © 2005 Matthew Shaw Illustrations © 2005 The British Library Board and other named copyright holders

British Library Cataloguing in Publication Data A catalogue record for this book is available from The British Library

ISBN 0 7123 4891 3

Designed and typeset by Andrew Barron @ thextension

Maps by Cedric Knight

Printed in Hong Kong by South Sea International Press

Contents

Introduction

Just to the east of the glorious and neo-Gothic Hunterian Museum of the
University of Glasgow the visitor can pass the blackened classical facade of
Wellington Church. Further east, Wellington and Waterloo Streets run across the
Victorian city's grid and outside the main library there stands a fine bronze statue
of the Duke astride his horse Copenhagen. At the opposite end of Britain, in
Broadstairs in Kent, where on a clear day France can be seen across the Channel,
the flint-lined streets have names such as Waterloo and Vimeiro, recalling the
names of Wellington's victories (and praising his wardenship of the Cinque Ports).
In London, Waterloo Bridge straddles the Thames, giving its name to the nearby
railway station and the less tactfully named point of departure for the Channel
Tunnel to France. More humbly, schoolchildren still pull on rubberized
Wellington boots to play in puddles or eat the sticky toffee and chocolate
of Wellington Squares. Restaurants of a traditional kind continue to serve
Beef Wellington. In Portugal, Wellington's desk is preserved in the museum
in Torres Vedras. These, and many more examples, suggest the imprint that
Arthur Wellesley (originally Wesley), 1st Duke of Wellington, made on British,
and indeed world, culture.

His career was founded on three great military triumphs. In India,
his campaigns mixed meticulous preparation with speed and ensured British
predominance in the sub-continent for well over a century; in the Iberian
peninsula, his steady military strategy and application of guerrilla warfare created
an 'ulcer' that drained troops from Napoleon's eastern campaigns; and in 1815 he
halted Napoleon's ambitions forever in the muddy fields of Waterloo. Wellington
was more than a general, and served as a public servant for almost forty years as a
statesman, prime minister and public figure. Although a Tory, he sought to avoid
partisanship; he opposed the Reform Bill of 1832, which extended the franchise

Previous page: *The Duke of Wellington*, oil painting by Sir Thomas Lawrence for Sir Robert Peel, 1824. Lawrence initially proposed painting Wellington with a pocket watch, but Wellington thought this might suggest that he was over-anxious for the Prussians' arrival at Waterloo. He protested to the artist that, 'That will never do. I was *not* waiting for the arrival of the Prussians at Waterloo. Put a telescope in my hand if you please.'
The Wellington College, Berkshire

to the middle classes, but fought hard for Catholic emancipation in Ireland in the face of party and popular opposition. Through his display of the virtues of determination, restraint and duty, he became for the Victorians an archetype of the heroic Englishman.

Today, the name of Wellington perhaps lacks the magnetism of his contemporaries Nelson or Napoleon. He did not die young, nor did he conquer a vast empire. His engagement with politics left him with many enemies, from the London mob to high society's liberal drawing rooms. Wellington was not mercurial or touched with startling genius, but won his victories through exacting preparation, determination and tactical brilliance. But just as Nelson was somewhat suspect to the Victorian mind — too flamboyant, too amorous — Wellington typified the stable qualities celebrated by the burghers of Glasgow when they laid out their mercantile city. Following his death in 1852, Wellington was perhaps the foremost in the Victorian pantheon of heroes — he was stoical, steady, brave, little given to hyperbole and dutiful, all qualities that have become less attractive in an age not as convinced by the qualities of duty or martial diligence. He stood for the military power of Britain, the solidity of Britishness in the face of foreign despotism and for the personal virtues of respectability, coolness and public service. Does this image stand up to scrutiny?

Wellington himself avoided histories of his victories, declaring that one might as well write a history of a ball as of a battle for all that it would tell you of the truth of such a confused affair, and he burnt much of his personal correspondence (advising others to do the same). He saw the need to present a sober public face, even though he did not shirk a number of romantic entanglements and a fondness for dancing, hunting and a certain amount of mischief (he also in later life created what amounts to a shrine to his victory over

Napoleon in Apsley House, his London home, which is stuffed with treasures,
paintings and a massive statue of the Emperor). Although a vast number of his
official dispatches and some personal correspondence have been printed (and
were avidly read in the nineteenth century) or survive in public or private
collections, his public image is in the main the result of published anecdotes
(many of which the Duke polished through countless retellings) and memoirs.
Such evidence is not always wholly unreliable, but it does cast a figure in a
certain polished light, with each retelling removing the sense of contingency,
imperfection and confusion of any life. This book pulls back some of these layers,
if only by presenting wherever possible in visual form the ways in which the
memory of Wellington has been preserved and, in some ways, created.

1

From Dublin to Mysore

The future Duke of Wellington was born in the spring of 1769 at Mornington House, Dublin. The baby boy was baptised at the family church, St Peter's, and named Arthur after his maternal grandfather. The evidence of the nursemaid, local papers and the baptismal record differ on the date of the birth: 6 March, and 3, 29 and 30 April are all proposed as possible dates, although Wellington always kept 1 May as his birthday. Whatever the exact date, Arthur was born into a heritage of service and status. The earliest mention of the Wellesley family can be found in a charter dating from 1180 in the library of Wells Cathedral in Somerset. It places Wellington's ancestry among the conquering elite of the Norman invasion as the family had been granted lands to the south of Wells around a settlement still known today as Wellesley Farm. Following Henry II's invasion of Ireland in the 1170s, in which the Wellesleys acted as standard bearer for the King, members of the family moved to the lands they had acquired in the counties of Kildare and Wexford, and purchased property in Dublin. The Wellesleys intermarried among fellow Anglo-Norman families, accumulated lands and held various important offices on behalf of the Crown. Sir William de Wellesley, for example, served as Keeper of the Castles of Kildare and Carbery, Justice of the Peace for Kildare and Kenny, Sheriff of Kildare and Member of Parliament in 1372. For six centuries, the family were part of a ruling caste, exacting obedience from the English monarch's Irish subjects, highly aware of their own status as members of a ruling elite.

The young Arthur's paternal grandfather was a Colley, an Anglo-Irish family with an ancestry comparable in its respectability to the Wellesleys. In 1728, he inherited a fortune along with the name Wesley from his cousin, Garrett Wesley. On his death, he bequeathed to his son the title of Lord Mornington, an interest in music and the expense of maintaining the family seat at Dangan Castle in

Previous page: *Arthur Wesley as Lieutenant-Colonel of the 33rd Foot* by John Hoppner, c.1795. Arthur's brother Richard thought the picture 'conveys the true expression of your countenance'. Arthur was about twenty-six years old. *Stratfield Saye. By permission of the trustees of the Duke of Wellington*

Below: Wellington's mother, Anne Wellesley, dowager Countess of Mornington, portrayed with busts of Wellington and his brothers Richard Colley Wellesley, Marquess Wellesley, and William Wellesley Pole, 3rd Earl of Mornington. She died in September 1831. The mezzotint is by Thomas Hodgetts, 1839. *National Portrait Gallery, London*

County Meath (which had been rebuilt and much improved during his lifetime by the addition of water gardens and a network of canals). Lord Mornington became a noted violinist and composer, was elected the first Professor of Music at the University of Dublin and was raised to an earldom in 1760. He was known for his melodic 'glees' (songs for three or more voices), particularly 'Here in cool grot', and sacred compositions (two of his settings for the psalms are still sung in churches and cathedrals), but his music-making did not provide well for the family, and the house at Dangan drained money. In the chill of February 1759, Lord Mornington married the sixteen-year-old Anne Hill, the eldest daughter of the future Lord Dungannon, but the alliance did not bring financial security. Anne possessed no inheritance of her own. Mornington provided her with £1,600 per annum, and £500 for her personal expenses. His new wife was thought to add some 'pepper' to the more relaxed Wellesley character. She grew to be a formidable woman, although described by some as somewhat 'cold and severe', and with her Wellington had a strained relationship.

Little is known of Wellington's childhood as a younger son of a large family; as an adult he himself referred infrequently to it, suggesting an unhappy youth, one that was overshadowed by showier, talented siblings. The family's expectations lay with Wellington's two older brothers, Richard (known also as Richard Colley) and William. Richard was brilliant, gifted in the study of Greek and Latin and excelling during his time at Harrow, Eton and Oxford; in 1797 he became Governor-General of India, with crucial implications for Wellington's career. There was also an older sister, Anne, and two younger brothers, Gerald Valerian and Henry. Two other children, Arthur and Francis, died in infancy.

Arthur's schooling began at the Diocesan School in Trim, County Meath, but in order to avoid the contemporary stigma of an Irish accent he was sent to Brown's, an English preparatory school in Chelsea. The family also moved to London, where Lord Mornington worked on his compositions, breakfasted weekly with the great (and unrelated) Methodist hymn writer, Charles Wesley, 'making music with all the Wesley children', and was noted as the first member of the aristocracy to be seen walking without shame through the streets of London while carrying a violin case. But in May 1781, Lord Mornington died. Richard left Oxford without a degree in order to attempt to settle the family's affairs.

That autumn, after losing his father, Arthur went to Eton College, perhaps the most aristocratic and prestigious school in the land. His time there was not happy. He recalled that he was 'a dreamy, idle and shy lad' and, possibly because of frequent ill health, avoided playground games. He also gained a lasting distaste for classical languages, in which he failed to excel, finding his younger brother Gerald overtaking him: in later life he made a point of avoiding all Latin phrases in public speaking. He did better with his mathematics. Socially, he made little impression and, by all accounts, the young man tended to keep to himself, playing alone (he later recalled that he used to amuse himself by repeatedly jumping a 'black ditch'), and only making a mark on his peers when he staged a fight with another pupil, Robert Percy 'Bobus' Smith, the brother of the wit and cleric, Sydney Smith. While Bobus was swimming, Arthur began to throw stones at him. He scrambled out of the river and began to fight his attacker, but Arthur had the better of him; the defeated Bobus later claimed: 'I was the Duke of Wellington's first victory.' It may also have been Arthur's attempt to find some recognition in the rough world of the schoolyard.

Although rough, Eton also provided an entrée to the highest levels of society. Arthur could count among his classmates the sons of three dukes, a marquess and thirteen earls, as well as a brace of offspring from other ranks of peer. Although the aphorism that the 'Battle of Waterloo was won on the playing-fields of Eton' derives from a misquotation from the French writer Montalembert rather than the future Duke of Wellington, the schoolyard did furnish many of his future senior officers and political allies and enemies. His contemporaries included Lord Holland and Earl Grey, later implacable Whig political opponents of the Duke of Wellington. ('Whigs' was the term for the political groups believing in the constitutional limits of the monarch. Their opponents were labelled 'Tories'.) The curriculum was also noted for its encouragement of brilliant scholars, including Arthur's brother Richard, and its schoolyard could count the future poet Percy Bysshe Shelley, and the future Prime Minister William Pitt.

Arthur did not flourish at Eton, and in 1784 he left to join his mother in Brussels, where she had moved to live more affordably. He was taught by a local lawyer; a fellow pupil commented on Arthur's fondness and aptitude for the fiddle. Two years later his mother resolved that her seventeen-year-old 'ugly boy'

Earl of Mornington, afterwards Marquess Wellesley by Robert Hume, c.1803. A portrait of Arthur's brilliant and ambitious elder brother, Richard. It is unlikely that Arthur would have held the positions that he did early in his career without Richard's patronage, as many contemporaries were keen to remark upon.
The British Library, Foster 2

EARL of MORNINGTON afterwards MARQUESS WELLESLEY
GOVERNOR GENERAL of BENGAL 1798 to 1805
*Presented in 1875 to the Secretary of State for India by
Sir H. C. MONTGOMERY, Bart. Member of Council.*
Painted by R. HOME

was 'food for powder and nothing more', and he was sent to the Royal Academy of Equitation at Angers in Anjou, France. Arthur was to be trained to serve as an officer in the British army: a not uncommon choice of career for a younger member of a lesser aristocratic family, but well short of the political career that was planned for his older brothers. The academy in Angers was a grand place, with a monumental classical facade and large courtyards. It had trained generations of Continental and British gentlemen, including the first Earl of Chatham (William Pitt, the elder), in the arts of fencing, horsemanship and mathematics, and aimed to give them a patina of social grace. There, Arthur continued to do well in mathematics (and in later life he had a good understanding of ballistics, if little sympathy for artillery), and improved his riding skills; although he never got over a poor riding position towards the back of the horse, which led to several falls during his many hours on the hunting field. He seems to have found the academy more congenial than either Eton or Brussels, falling in with two other sons of Irish peers, with whom he took to loitering in the city's cafes and inns with French officers, or playing cards with the wife of the academy's principal. Although he was often unwell and spent hours alone, the trio were also noted for mild pranks such as dropping coins from the academy's windows on passers-by. He also mixed with French nobility, and was introduced to the Abbé Siéyès (the future French revolutionary pamphleteer and statesman) and later claimed to have come across Chateaubriand, the romantic writer. Wellington also gained a lifelong taste for France and a good grasp of the French tongue, albeit with a Belgian accent.

He returned to London in late 1786, no longer the shy, sickly child, but a well-groomed and more confident young man, 'handsome, fashioned tall and elegant' according to some well-to-do 'aunts'. His brother Richard obtained a commission for him as an ensign in the 73rd Foot in March 1787. The regiment was safely posted in India and, agreeably, there was no immediate call for him to join it. Drawing on his brother's patronage and his mother's letter-writing, Arthur was appointed as aide-de-camp to the Lord Lieutenant of Ireland in Dublin in the autumn of that year. This role as confidential assistant to the Lord Lieutenant required him to attend government meetings at Dublin Castle and provided a useful extra ten shillings a day and an excuse for not joining his regiment overseas. On Christmas Day, he was promoted to lieutenant in the 76th Foot. In January 1788, he transferred to the 41st Foot and then in June moved to the 12th Light Dragoons, avoiding a posting to the East Indies and, possibly, an early grave from tropical disease. He obtained a captaincy in the 58th Foot in 1791, and transferred the next year to the 18th Light Dragoons. Such moves among regiments were not uncommon; indeed, it was the usual means by which a military career could be advanced and pay increased. Arthur's family connections eased the process, which required both cash and networks of patronage. Similarly, Arthur made use of his family's standing to embark on a political career, and from 1790, he represented the family borough of Trim in the Irish Parliament.

Having reached the age of majority, Arthur was living an unremarkable life, typical of many younger sons of the Anglo-Irish aristocracy. He was making his way slowly, but surely, in the corrupt, self-serving and provincial world of Irish politics, and thanks to his family connections had secured a reasonable position in the army. Money remained something of a problem, and he was forced to borrow (despite his later claims that he had never been in debt) to supplement his officer's pay. Like many men of his age and times, he enjoyed cards and other entertainments; he also showed an enthusiasm for fine tailoring and, if not flamboyant dress, then a flair for style, choosing coats of a satisfying blue and boots

Kitty, Viscountess Wellington, drawn by John Slater, 1811. Wellington soon realised that his marriage to Kitty was a mistake, and spent most of his time apart from her. In 1821, his threats of a separation caused her to consider suicide.
Stratfield Saye. By permission of the trustees of the Duke of Wellington

of expensive leather. (His first nickname as a general was to be 'The Beau'.)

Arthur was now able to contemplate marriage. For some time, he had courted Kitty Pakenham, a well-known member of Dublin society and sister to the eighteen-year-old Lord Longford. They were in love, but Arthur's situation was too lowly to propose. He wrote to Richard asking for money to purchase a higher commission; in April 1793, he became a major in the 33rd Foot. But still this was not enough to satisfy Kitty's brother, and Arthur faced a humiliating refusal to his marriage proposal from a man almost six years his junior. The refusal can be seen as a turning point in Arthur's life, and a new sense of resolve and ambition can be detected in him. Like his father, Arthur was fond of playing the violin, but in the summer of 1793 he placed his instrument in a fire, never playing again. The fiddle was unsuitable for an officer, and perhaps he also saw where such leisurely attractions might lead him, having watched his father waste the family fortune and position in his musical pursuits. He began to study for several hours a day and wrote to his brother asking for another post, but this time away from Dublin and in service abroad. Nothing immediately came of this request, but in the spring of 1794, Arthur's regiment was to be sent abroad to defend the Belgian ports from the advances of the French Republican armies. He wrote a farewell to Kitty: 'As Lord Longford's determination is founded upon prudential motives and may be changed should my situation be altered before I return to Ireland, I hope you will believe that should anything occur which may induce you and him to change your minds, my mind will remain the same.'

By the end of the 1780s, France had failed to resolve a series of financial crises, and King Louis XVI and his advisers determined to call a meeting of the three 'estates' of France (the clergy, the nobility and the 'Third Estate' of commoners) thereby turning a financial crisis into a political one. In accordance with tradition, villages and institutions across France prepared a 'statement of grievances' to be sent to the King; rumours of reform and of foreign plots began to spread, and in July 1789, discontent broke into open revolt. In Versailles, representatives of the Third Estate refused to leave the King's Tennis Court (to where they had decamped following their exclusion from their assigned meeting hall) until France was provided with a constitution; in Paris, a mob stormed the Bastille prison, and the countryside soon erupted in waves of violence. The French Revolution had begun.

Initially, the events in France were welcomed by many in Britain who believed the French were experiencing a revolution comparable to theirs of 1688, but as the Revolution became more radical − clergy and aristocrats were exiled or fled, the King was put on trial, and 'government by terror' forever linked the Revolution to the guillotine − it was vilified and by 1792 the British government began to suppress all signs of sedition. Austria and Prussia, disgusted at the treatment of Louis and Marie Antoinette, his Austrian wife, rallied behind the émigré French royalty and declared war on the Republic. However, the ideological import of the Revolution – the promise of liberty, equality and fraternity; the language of rights and republicanism – spread through Europe, threatening the existing monarchical regimes. France also began to draw upon new military thinking, deploying large numbers of committed troops in new formations, particularly combinations of massed columns of troops fronted by skirmishers, which through force of numbers and ferocity could smash through traditional infantry lines. These new, mass armies could also live off the land, unlike their enemies, and did not require extensive supply lines. Militarily and ideologically, the balance of power in Europe had been destroyed, and the Continent had entered a period of almost continual war, only ended by the settlement at the great Congress of Vienna in 1815. The future Duke of Wellington opposed both the republican ideas and the military might of the Revolution.

In 1794, after rebuffing the attacking Saxe-Coburg army at Tourcoing (near Lille), the French had pressed north and occupied Belgium. In June, the 33rd Foot, along with Colonel Arthur Wesley, sailed from Cork to Ostend to defend the North Sea ports. It was to be his first experience of active service; it was also to be a first-hand encounter with defeat and disaster. He had been warned by an old colonel that active service was a trial: 'You little know what you are going to meet with. You will often have no dinner at all. I mean literally no dinner, and not merely roughing it on a beefsteak or a bottle of wine.' Although correct, the warning underestimated the trial of the campaign through the bitter Dutch winter, with troops freezing on the road, cut off from supplies of food or clothes. Arthur's part in the expedition showed a fair amount of skill and common sense, but the adventure, directed from the Horse Guards in London, revealed the dismal state of the British army: poorly trained, relying on techniques unchanged for generations and with some equipment equally as venerable. The expedition showed Britain's poor military condition in the face of a committed military threat; for Arthur, the experience was invaluable, in that it showed him how not to lead a campaign and drove home the importance of supplies and of marshalling meticulous preparation.

Arthur commanded three battalions and oversaw the prudent evacuation of Ostend in the face of a vigorous French advance, before landing again at Antwerp. The alliance began to fall apart; the Austrians withdrew to the east, and the British, underfed and ill-equipped, began a miserable retreat through Holland. In September, Arthur saw battle for the first time when he commanded his brigade in a small confrontation at Boxtel, ensuring that the British line held in the face of the French advance. The retreat continued through the winter, until the British held the line at the frozen River Waal. Here, Arthur acted in near total independence from higher command, noting later that 'I was on the Waal, I think, from October to January, and during all that time I only saw once one General from the headquarters.' The only diversion came during the day, when the French, were 'perpetually chattering with our officers and soldiers, and danc[ing] the *carmagnole* upon the opposite bank; but occasionally the spectators on our side are interrupted in the middle of a dance by a cannon ball from ours.' In March, he returned to England. He had seen how a British line could resist French troops and, perhaps more importantly, witnessed how distant leadership could cause an army to disintegrate. It taught him 'what one ought not to do, and that is always something'.

Once back in Dublin, he began to petition for some form of promotion. This was not forthcoming, so he turned his attention to civil patronage, setting his sights on the Irish Revenue. In the autumn, his regiment was to be sent to

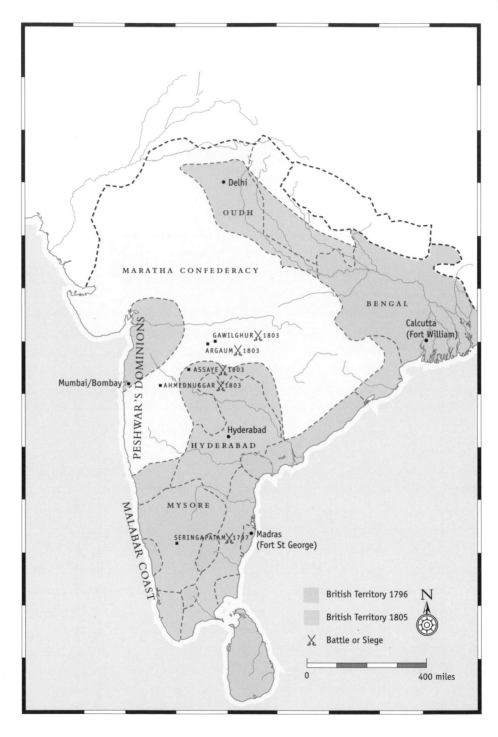

Delhi

OUDH

MARATHA CONFEDERACY

BENGAL

Calcutta
(Fort William)

GAWILGHUR ✕ 1803
ARGAUM ✕ 1803

ASSAYE ✕ 1803
AHMEDNUGGAR ✕ 1803

Mumbai/Bombay

PESHWAR'S DOMINIONS

Hyderabad

HYDERABAD

MALABAR COAST

MYSORE

SERINGAPATAM ✕ 1797

Madras
(Fort St George)

British Territory 1796

British Territory 1805

✕ Battle or Siege

N

0   400 miles

Opposite: Map showing battles of
Arthur Wellesley during the Indian
campaigns, 1797–1805.

Below: *The Bengal Levee*, hand-coloured
etching by James Gillray, 1792. The
potential profits to be made in India
created a culture of corruption and
sycophancy. This etching shows
Lord Cornwallis, who established the
Cornwallis (or 'Bengal') code in an
attempt to reform these excesses,
surrounded by a crowd of such men.
The British Library, P1001

the Caribbean; indeed, Arthur set sail in December, but was blown back to port
by storms in February, 1796. But before he succeeded in either finding suitable
employment or successfully sailing to the West Indies, the government decided
that his regiment was to be sent to India.

The India in which Colonel Wesley arrived after a three-month journey
was a kaleidoscope of competing powers. Since the decline of the Mogul Empire,
a patchwork of sultans, maharajahs and warlords ruled the subcontinent. At first,
the Western powers had been restricted to small trading posts on the coasts,
known as factories or presidencies, but by the mid-eighteenth century, British
and French trading companies had begun to expand into the interior, operating

client states and claiming other territories as their own. By the end of the
century, the British presence in India consisted of three presidencies (Bombay in
the west, Madras to the south and Bengal in the east), under the dual control of
the British Crown and the private East India Company. France also exercised
a strong influence through its trading posts and controlled Mauritius, while
Portugal retained a presence in Goa in the west. Beyond India, in the Far East,
the Dutch and French controlled much of the Javan trade.

For Europeans, India was both a treasure trove and a graveyard. Great
fortunes could be made – the first Governor-General, Warren Hastings,
accumulated a personal fortune of some £200,000 – but as a result of disease
(and, often, hard living), life expectancy for new arrivals could be as short as two
years. Unlike many of his fellow officers, Colonel Wesley escaped serious illness,
but his Mysore dispatches are not lacking in references to stomach complaints,
ague, colds and other ailments. Also, unlike many of his fellow Britons, he vowed
to avoid the excesses of drink, taking only a bottle of wine a day at a time when
three was considered the minimum.

Before Arthur left London, he had spent £50 on a library to take with him.
The volumes were heavily weighted towards books on India, but he included
general history and military matters, together with works by Adam Smith and
Jonathan Swift, and the campaigns of Caesar – in which he found many
similarities to campaigning in India. Chapman's *Venereal Disease* speaks of his
concern for the health of the members of his regiment. Part of his £50 also
went on Rousseau's *Nouvelle Héloïse* and nine volumes of the sentimental *Women
of Pleasure*. The library was practical and realistic, and showed an intelligent,
open mind that respected the pleasures offered by reading. Most of the volumes
followed him during his travels around India: he appears, though, to have

disposed of Plutarch and *Women of Pleasure*. He also included James Mackintosh's *Vindiciæ Gallicæ*, a vigorous defence of the French Revolution in the face of the attacks in Edmund Burke's *Reflections on the Revolution in France*. He continued to purchase books during his stay in India.

Almost immediately after his arrival, Arthur again set sail. Britain was now at war with Spain and Holland, and the 33rd was despatched to capture Manila in the Philippines. Arthur made detailed plans for the invasion and gave careful instructions for the hygiene of his troops, but it proved to be yet another aborted mission, and the regiment was recalled at Penang. His arrival back at Calcutta in November brought the welcome news that his eldest brother, Richard, had been appointed Governor-General of India; another Wesley brother, Henry, was appointed as Richard's private secretary. The appointment boded well for Arthur's prospects, and he had the satisfaction of knowing that he had played a crucial role in persuading his brother to petition for the post. It also marked the ambition and confidence of the Wesley clan, and was a tribute to its political nous. On Richard's arrival, Arthur took the cue from his brother and adopted the more expansive surname of Wellesley.

Richard considered the position of Governor-General as 'the most distinguished situation in the British Empire after that of the Prime Minister of England' and recognized the vast potential for British expansion in the subcontinent. He quickly co-opted Arthur as his unofficial adviser on military matters, despite his relative inexperience, and the opportunity for expansion soon arose. First, the Nizam of Hyderabad, whose realm stretched across the heart of India, fell under British influence thanks to a coup against the French party. Then Richard planned to subdue Tipu Sultan, the daring 'Tiger of Mysore' in the north-west. Tipu had seized the mainly Hindu state of Mysore, and although

Opposite: Tipu Sultan, ruler of the Kingdom of Mysore (1782–1799), 1792. Through a series of alliances, including with the French, Tipu Sultan helped to check British advances in India. Known as the 'Tiger of Mysore' he made use of French military tactics and introduced liberal reforms. He died at the siege of Seringapatam in 1799.
The British Library, Foster 28

defeated by Lord Cornwallis in the Second Mysore War of 1790–1792, he had retained his independence and allied himself with the French. In Europe, the young general Napoleon Bonaparte had led the French to victory in Italy and now in Egypt, and rumours of French alliances in India began to disquiet the British. An attack on Tipu could be seen as pre-empting French expansion, while the Tipu's poor treatment of prisoners provided a moral justification (notoriously, he kept captives chained in a dungeon up to their necks in water). Arthur and his regiment were sent to north-east Madras to prepare for operations against him. Arthur was unconvinced of the military danger posed by Tipu, but deferred to his brother's authority. He had the opportunity to test his political skills, as he had to persuade Lord Clive, the Governor of Madras and son of Clive of India, of the need to go to war, and his diplomatic skills were in evidence when he advised Richard not to join the army, for fear of undermining the general's authority.

It became clear that the British would act against Tipu. Following the death of his senior officer in a duel, Arthur was appointed senior adviser to Mir Allum, the commander of the Nizam of Hyderabad's forces (which included six East India Company infantry battalions and, following Arthur's appointment, the 33rd Foot). The appointment led to jealous sniping. Years after the campaign, several officers remained bitter at Arthur's role in the campaign, perceiving him as having benefited from nepotism, even though the Nizam's prime minister had requested him.

The campaign would prove formative for Arthur. General George Harris, who had overall command of the campaign, marched from the west and Arthur's columns marched from the east accompanied by 120,000 bullocks, and harassed by Tipu's light cavalry en route. They converged at Tipu's fortified town of Seringapatam. On 26 March, in the thick jungle around Malavelly, the army confronted Tipu's, which included elephants and rocket artillerymen. The next

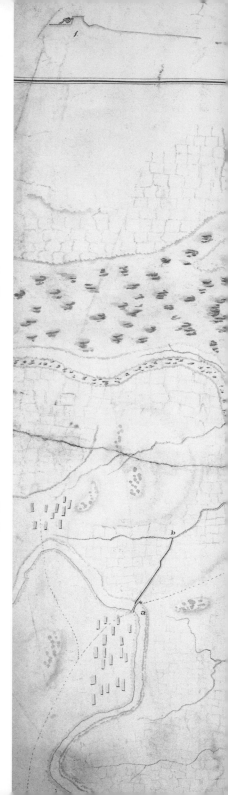

Plan of Attack of the Fort of Seringapatam, belonging to Marquess Wellesley. The siege of the fortress followed the classical European rules of siege warfare, as laid out by Sébastien de Vauban in the seventeenth century, with a formal series of batteries, parallels (trenches) and zigzags (connecting lines) before the final breach. Wellesley was in charge of the reserves.
The British Library, Add. MS. 13906 C

day, the 33rd held its line against the advance of 2,000 of Tipu's men in column, and the Allies moved two miles to the west of the city. Although Arthur wrote to his brother assuring him of success, the encounter was a difficult one, with Tipu's well-trained men carefully concealed in jungle thickets. Harris ordered Arthur to clear a copse by the village of Sultanpettah. The 33rd attacked that night, but Arthur's men became confused in the dense jungle and were slowed down by waterlogged ditches and fierce hand-to-hand fighting. Tipu's troops dispersed the attack. Arthur, exhausted and wounded in the leg by a spent musket ball, returned to camp to report on his failure. Twelve soldiers were captured by Tipu's men and killed by strangulation or by nails through the skull, and several of Arthur's closest friends from Ireland died in the course of the action. The enemy was swiftly defeated on the morning of 6 April, with Arthur leading the charge, but the setback profoundly unsettled the young colonel. He resolved never to attack at night again without proper preparations; his enemies were already spreading stories of how he had been found

Section through the Face Attacked

1. Flag Staff & Cavalier. — 2. Breaching Battery.

Plan of Attack
of the
Fort of Seringapatam
taken by Storm on the 4th May 1799
by the Army under the Command of
Lieut. Genl. George Harris

References.

a	Shaw's Post
b	MacDonald's Post
c	Powder Mill
d	Approaches & Intrenchments
e	Battery to fire upon the Enemy's Intrenchm.
fff	Batteries to take off the Defences
gg	Breaching Batteries
h	Batteries to favor the Assault
i	Enemy's Intrenchments

Scale of Yards

asleep with his head on the mess table, and saying that 'Wellesley is mad'. Years later, he could still bitterly recall the exact details of the engagement.

On 6 May, the Allies took the fortress of Seringapatam after a two-day siege. Tipu Sultan died in the defence of the North Gate, and an orgy of looting by the British was then unleashed. An amulet on Tipu's arm was recognized in a pile of corpses, and his still warm body was pulled out. Arthur felt the pulse expire. General David Baird, who had led the charge on the fortress, was relieved from command in order to rest and Arthur was installed as acting Governor of Seringapatam. Baird was furious, but he was unpopular with the natives (he had been held as prisoner in the city before and could be expected to exact revenge). Arthur later recalled in conversation with John Wilson Croker, Secretary to the Admiralty, that 'I was the *fit person* to be selected. I had commanded the Nizam's army during the campaign, and had given universal satisfaction. I was liked by the natives.' In contrast, 'Baird was a gallant, hard-headed, lion-hearted officer, but he had no talent, no tact' and 'had strong prejudices against the natives'.

Arthur received £4,000 in prize money: the treasure removed from the city was later estimated at £1,143,216, and £4,000 by no means covered his expenses. As commander, he was expected to entertain his officers (he was required to commission a dinner service of tureens and serving plates) and had debts to settle with his brother; Richard deferred payment. Arthur was also confronted with the problem of restoring order in the city (he hanged looters as an example), and bringing peace to the surrounding countryside through deft deployment of light troops. Although he endeavoured to see that justice was administered properly, such mopping-up operations no doubt involved harsh repression. He also worked with local customs, allowing Hindu and Muslim codes of law to operate, and refusing to free Christian prisoners on the basis of their religion. He proved himself to be an excellent and diligent administrator; he may also have learnt of the effectiveness of guerrilla warfare as the remainder of Tipu's men hid and fought in the surrounding countryside, something that he recalled in Portugal and Spain. Finally, in September 1800, he destroyed the 5,000-strong army of Dhoondiah Waugh, a warlord who had escaped from Tipu's jungle; he undertook to take care of Dhoondiah's five-year-old son, who was found after his father was killed. The battle also marked the final time that Colonel Wellesley personally led a cavalry charge. His star was rising, his military competence was recognized, and he seemed set for his own command.

In November 1800, his brother, who had been elevated as the Marquess of Wellesley (although only in the Irish peerage – he dubbed the marquessate a 'double-gilt potato'), devised a plan to secretly dispatch Arthur at the head of an army heading to Ceylon, from where he would capture the Île de France (Mauritius) and become Commander-in-Chief of the Isles of France and Bourbon. Arthur was enthusiastic: finally, he was to have his own command. But when he reached Ceylon, a letter from Richard informed him that he might instead have to attack the French in Egypt. Such an expedition called for a general as commander, not a mere colonel like him. Richard avoided making a final decision, and he returned in fury without orders to Bombay in March 1801. He ceased all direct communication with Richard for the best part of a year. He wrote to his brother Henry: 'I was at the top of the tree in this country ... But this supersession has ruined all my prospects.' In the end, illness kept him in India: he succumbed to a painful condition known as the Malabar itch (a form of ringworm), and undertook a series of painful acid baths as a cure. He resigned himself to go to Egypt under the command of General Baird, but a fever prevented him. In the end, he retained his command in Mysore.

Tipu's Tiger. The mechanical tiger
belonging to Tipu Sultan could be
made to growl as it appeared to devour
a British officer. Arthur presented it as
a gift to his brother Richard, following
the capture of Seringapatam.
Victoria and Albert Museum, 2545(IS)

In April 1802, he received promotion to the rank of major general, and in November he was sent to conquer the Marathas in central India, whose state had long been under French influence and was now in a state of civil war. He restored the Peshwa of the Marathas (the titular chief of the region, who had accepted British protection) through a meticulously managed swift march from Mysore, and attempted to persuade French-allied enemy armies of Daulat Rāu Scindia, Maharajah of Gwalior, and the Bohnsle of Berar to disarm. He failed, and on 6 August 1803, war was declared. First, the hill fortress of Ahmednuggar was captured. The Maratha chief was reported as saying, 'These English are a strange people. They came here in the morning, surveyed the wall, walked over it, killed the garrison and returned to breakfast.' It was an easy victory that perhaps led Arthur to later underestimate the difficulty of siege warfare in Europe.

Arthur resolved to bring the enemy to a decisive battle, and marched inland. In September, his force of 5,000 found Scindia's entire French-trained army arranged across a plain, with the village of Assaye on their east and a river protecting their front. Scindia's army was around 40,000 men. Arthur had twenty-two cannon, compared to Scindia's hundred or so, but he made decisive use of his ability to read the ground tactically. He decided to attack (he was not the purely defensive general that some of his critics have made out), calculating that there must be a ford to be found across the river and that the ground would then favour the attackers, since he would provide no room for what Arthur deemed 'the overwhelming deluge of native cavalry'.

Scindia's army responded to the attack with a swift manoeuvre, aptly demonstrating the troops' high level of training. Soon, the cannon were facing the direction of Arthur's attack. He adjusted his flank, writing that he 'attacked them immediately… the troops advanced under a very hot fire from the cannon, the

execution of which was terrible.' The British overran the guns, and the enemy
infantry quickly fell back. But on the right, the 74th Foot and the pickets were
almost destroyed by the remaining guns. The reserve 19th Dragoons and 4th
Native Cavalry had been brought forward by Arthur, and they charged to save the
flank. The Marathas were pushed back decisively, and although many of the enemy
escaped, the victory was total. It was a very close-run thing. The Marathas suffered
some 1,200 killed and 4,800 wounded; the British and native troops lost 1,584.
Arthur himself lost two horses under him, and woke that night after having a
nightmare – 'a confused notion that they were *all* killed'. It was, he recalled, the
'bloodiest for the numbers that I ever saw'.

The Battle of Assaye was seen as a triumph by the British. Arthur was now
famous. More campaigning followed, ending with another victory at Argaum, but
by 1804, Arthur was again thinking of Europe, 'anxious to a degree which I can't
express to see my friends again.' India had been his education, but now it was
time to return home. He had made his name and no little fortune (the spoils
of war netted him around £40,000, making him a millionaire in today's terms),
but while promotion was promised, nothing was forthcoming. He had become
an experienced commander and administrator, and had displayed his tactical
brilliance and ability for meticulous planning, but Richard was to be replaced as
Governor-General in June 1805, and Arthur could see little but continual war
and vast expense ahead as the East India Company expanded its Indian empire.
On 8 June 1804, he applied for leave to return home, and finally set sail for
England on 10 March 1805, on board HMS *Trident*. As was usual, the ship visited
St Helena, which he found to be a remarkably healthful island, and was, of
course, to be the final, inescapable prison for Napoleon. Arthur also had
unfinished business in Dublin: Kitty was waiting.

2

The fatal knot

While in India, Arthur had continued to correspond with his Dublin friends, although not directly with Kitty. One correspondent, Mrs Sparrow, resurrected these ties, and on his return to Europe he proposed to Kitty again, recalling his commitment to her. This time, Arthur was rich and had been made a member of the Order of the Bath, giving him the title 'Sir Arthur'. The family could hardly refuse him, although Kitty suggested that they should meet before finalizing any agreement, since she had aged and was 'much changed'. Sir Arthur would have none of this, claiming that he cared only for the person within, not her appearance, and in April 1807 he headed to Dublin for their wedding. Perhaps regretting his decision, he is said to have whispered ungallantly to his brother Gerard before the ceremony, 'She has grown ugly, by Jove.'

The marriage was a curious affair, and must have appeared so to contemporaries, even in an age when marriages were as much a matter of practical calculation as of love. Arthur had left Ireland a young man, returning a mature thirty-six-year-old, with experience not only of leading men, but of mixing with and enjoying the company of women. Indeed, he was noted within his Indian set as having a fondness for other officers' wives, and like most men of his position, visited the more reputable sort of bawdy-house. He once drily proposed giving 'from Goklah a famous whore who had belonged to Dhoondiah … as a present to her Native Town'. On his way through London, he called on Mrs Porter, the society procuress, where he probably enjoyed the company of the courtesan Harriette Wilson. (Later, discreet rumours of mistresses in Spain hinted at liaisons outside his marriage, and he continued to enjoy the company of intelligent, self-assured women, such as the heiress Lady Frances Shelley, and Harriet Arbuthnot, the wife of the British Ambassador in Paris.) Despite these flirtations and relationships, he strenuously avoided any public sexual scandal, in

Previous page: Harriet Arbuthnot,
the wife of the politician Charles
Arbuthnot, became a close friend of
Wellesley, acting as his 'social
secretary' in London. Engraved by
W. Giller after Sir Thomas Lawrence.
Mary Evans Picture Library

contrast to his elder brother, Lord Wellesley. For her part, Kitty remained devoted – and rather fearful of him.

On 12 September 1805, Sir Arthur visited Lord Castlereagh, the Secretary of State for War and the Colonies, in Downing Street. While he waited in an ante-room, he noticed a naval officer, whom he recognized from 'his pictures and the loss of an arm'. It was Lord Nelson. At first, Sir Arthur recalled, Nelson talked to him in a 'style so vain and silly as to surprise me and almost disgust me' before the Admiral briefly slipped out of the room 'no doubt to ask who I was' and then the future victor of Trafalgar behaved in 'altogether a different manner' towards the victor of Assaye. Sir Arthur visited Castlereagh several times in the following weeks and went riding with William Pitt, the Prime Minister. His opinion was sought on an over-ambitious scheme for two fleets simultaneously converging on Mexico, one approaching from the Caribbean, the other circumnavigating the globe, capturing Malay and the Philippines en route. Sir Arthur suggested that a single fleet and contingent of marines might be a less risky proposition. He was also present at Pitt's speech at the Guildhall in London following Nelson's triumph and death at Trafalgar, when Pitt responded to the toast 'The Saviour of the Nation' with 'Europe is not to be saved by any single man. England has saved herself by her exertions; and will, I trust, save Europe by her example.'

This example would be slow in coming. In December 1805, Sir Arthur was sent to command a reserve brigade during the British invasion of Bremen in Hanover; to European eyes, his victories in India did not warrant a greater command. Along with his troops, he spent three weeks on rough seas, before disembarking and enduring six cold, damp and disease-ridden weeks. He returned to take command of the south-coast defences at Hastings. Britain was no longer under threat of invasion and the posting was unsatisfying for a man of ambition. In October 1806 he wrote to Lord Grenville, the Prime Minister, seeking to 'serve with some of the European armies'; as he told his brother, he was 'very sorry to stay at home when others went abroad.'

Political service also took up his time. The constituents of Rye, Sussex, had elected him to the House of Commons in April 1806, where he was active in defending Richard from political attacks on his behaviour as Governor General in India. (He would later represent Mitchell, Cornwall, and Newport, Isle of Wight.) In March 1807, he accepted the position of Chief Secretary for Ireland on condition that he could leave his post if a command became available and, accompanied by Kitty and his one-month-old son, Arthur Richard, he returned to Dublin Castle. He found Ireland troubled: following the Irish Rebellion of 1798, British rule had been even more harshly imposed, and in 1800 the Irish Parliament voted for its own abolition, leading to Irish union with Great Britain as the United Kingdom of Great Britain and Ireland in 1801. Sir Arthur, a son of the Anglo-Irish elite, took the view that no compromise was possible, since the Irish would be satisfied with nothing short of independence – an anathema to his conception of a United Kingdom. The Irish were to be 'kept down by main force' if necessary, although he preferred 'mildness and good temper' when possible. His main task was the distribution of patronage, buying support with sinecures and other rewards; the experience of Irish politics confirmed his Tory views that while the methods of British rule could not be defended 'in the abstract', he believed that in practice they worked, forming a bond between the two nations.

By the summer of 1807, the British feared that the French would seize the neutral Danish fleet, making an invasion of Britain possible. The British demanded that the Danish cede their fleet to them, and launched an expedition

The Plumb-pudding in dang..
"the great Globe itself and all which it inher..

_State Epicures taking un Petit Souper .
too small to satisfy such insatiable appetites.
vide Mr W_d _ s eccentricities my Political Regret

Previous pages: *The Plum Pudding in Danger*, by James Gillray, 1805. William Pitt and Napoleon divide the world between themselves, although the 'great globe' proves to be 'too small to satisfy such insatiable appetites'. The Revolutionary and Napoleonic wars were global in scope and Britain considered striking against Napoleon's allies as far afield as Venezuela. Wellesley was cautious of 'revolutionizing any country for a political object... do not stir them up it is a fearful responsibility'. *The British Library, 745.a.6*

to ensure that they would. Sir Arthur had persuaded the Secretary of War to allow him to accompany the British force, although only as commander of the reserve, with an experienced second-in-command called Stewart (Sir Arthur called him a 'dry nurse') appointed by the Horse Guards to look after a man they viewed (in Sir Arthur's words) as merely a 'Lord's son, "a *sprig of nobility*" who came into the army more for ornament than use'. Steward disembarked the troops, and was quickly informed by Sir Arthur that ''Tis my turn now', who then took control of the forces. He soon demonstrated that he could successfully command a force on the Continent, dealing with a Danish force at Køge on 29 August. Following a British bombardment, Copenhagen surrendered in September, and General Sir Arthur returned to Dublin.

That spring, he learnt that he was to lead a 9,000-strong force to Venezuela to challenge the Spanish (who were allies of France), again leaving Kitty, who had given birth to a second son, Charles. But with his troops on board their vessels, the news of risings in the Asturias in north Spain and against the French garrison in Madrid reached Britain. Portugal had continued to trade with Britain, contravening the Continental System, and in 1807 Napoleon had ordered General Andoche Junot to invade; Lisbon was captured on 30 November, a day after the Portuguese royal family had fled to Brazil on board a ship of the Royal Navy. The French army also occupied areas of northern Spain, precipitating the flight and abdication of the Spanish King, Carlos IV. Napoleon speedily took advantage of the political crisis and placed his brother Joseph on the Spanish throne. But before Joseph could be crowned, the 1808 Spanish revolt – known as the 'Dos de Mayo' – began. Soon Spanish and Portuguese representatives arrived in London asking for assistance. Along with others, Sir Arthur immediately saw the opportunity to strike at Napoleon, and argued that his force should be sent to the Iberian peninsula instead of Venezuela. Although London hopes of a Bourbon restoration in France had faded, an attack on French influence in the Peninsula would be a warning against Napoleon's European ambitions and assist British trade. Sir Arthur's fleet would now sail to Portugal.

Before setting sail, he gave thought to the task ahead of him and the French armies he would face, ruminating about his opponents at a farewell dinner with Kitty (who had not been told of the scheme until it was certain) and Croker that: 'My die is cast, they may overwhelm me, but I don't think that will out-manoeuvre me. First, because I am not afraid of them, as everybody else seems to be; and secondly, because if what I hear of their system of manoeuvre is true, I think it a false one as against steady troops.' The campaign was to prove long and arduous, but in 1814, British troops would be marching from Spain into France.

At the age of thirty-nine, Sir Arthur was young to receive such a command, and he was given another 'dry nurse', General Sir Brent Spencer. Sir Arthur quickly told him that 'I did not know what the words "*second in command*" meant, any more than third, fourth, or fifth in command … I alone commanded the army.' But on 30 July, when Sir Arthur arrived at Mondego Bay where the troops were to land in Portugal, he received a letter marked 'Secret' from Castlereagh, once more Secretary of State for War. The French forces under the admittedly mediocre General Junot were more numerous than previously thought, and Sir Arthur's force was to be supplemented by 5,000 men under the brilliant and popular Sir John Moore. Disappointingly for Sir Arthur, his lack of seniority – and no doubt the Duke of York's personal dislike for him – had led the Horse Guards (the headquarters of the British army) to pass the command of the expedition to Lieutenant General Sir Hew Dalrymple (the Governor of

Gibraltar), with Lieutenant General Sir Harry Burrard as second in command. Sir Arthur was to press on with an attack against Lisbon while these officers sailed to Portugal; he hoped to beat Junot 'before any of them arrive'.

His troops began to land on 1 August in the dangerous surf off Mondego. It took a week for them to disembark fully. Sir Arthur then met the Portuguese general, Bernadino Freire, with his army of 6,000. The Allies decided that the Portuguese would march through the mountains, and Sir Arthur, together with 1,700 light Portuguese troops, would advance along the coast within reach of his support ships; both would head to Lisbon. As the historian Philip Guedalla noted, 'this southward thrust brought the French swarming out of Lisbon like angry wasps'. The British first clashed with this swarm on 14 August when a group of riflemen ran into some French soldiers at a windmill at Brilos. The French retreated, followed by the detachment of riflemen, who then ran into the French rearguard and had to be rescued by more British troops. An officer was killed, and Sir Arthur's brother-in-law, Captain Hercules Pakenham, was slightly wounded.

The French army, under General Henri Delaborde, now arranged itself in front of the hamlet of Roliça. They numbered around 4,000 compared to Sir Arthur's 10,700. Sir Arthur resolved to make use of his superior numbers and attack before a second French army arrived. On 17 August, he sent three columns towards the French, intending to distract the enemy with the central column and surround them with the other columns. But Delaborde saw through this gambit and quickly withdrew to a higher ground behind the hamlet. Before Sir Arthur could rearrange his troops, the 29th Foot advanced up a gully, and found themselves behind the French lines, who cut them to pieces: the battle had swung in the French army's favour. Seeing the danger, Sir Arthur immediately threw as many men as he could into a general attack, and Delaborde was pushed

'Battle of Vimeira' [*sic*], etched by
W. Heath, 1819. Sir Arthur
demonstrated that well-led British
troops could withstand the shock
of a massed French attack.
The British Library, 838.m.7

back. After it became clear that French reinforcements would not arrive in time, Delaborde ordered a well-executed retreat, leaving nearly 700 dead and three cannons. It was, Sir Arthur noted, a 'most desperate' battle. He lost 487 men.

On the 20th, Sir Harry Burrard arrived at the coast, along with 4,000 men. Sir Arthur was rowed out to him and attempted to convince him to march swiftly on Mafra, the next important town north of Lisbon. Sir Harry preferred to wait on board his ill-named ship, the *Brazen*, until Sir John Moore's troops arrived, and Sir Arthur returned to shore. But that night, with Sir Arthur still in command of the army, news of a surprise advance from the east by Junot arrived. Sir Arthur swiftly redeployed his men, who had been facing south, displaying an apparent coolness in the face of confusion. Showing a keen sense for the tactical possibilities of the ground, he placed the majority of his men on a ridge to the east of the Maceira Gorge (where the troops had landed), ordering them to lie down out of the French view. To the south of this ridge, he drew up lines to the east of a low hill known as Vimeiro, with reserves to the north and along the western ridge of the gorge.

The French advanced in four massed columns, screened by hundreds of *tirailleurs* (skirmishers). Sir Arthur matched these with his own riflemen, and the French were met with rifle-fire, shot and shrapnel from his twelve cannons and, at the last minute, a sharp, deadly volley from lines of well-drilled infantry. The French attempted to move from column into line so that they could match the British musket-fire, but the force of enemy shot and the difficulty of manoeuvring on the hill broke their ranks, and after bayonet fighting they retreated in confusion down the hill. Two further columns met the same fate. Burrard then arrived, and seeing the situation, allowed Sir Arthur to continue in command. But the day was not without its setbacks: Sir Arthur ordered the 20th (Light) Dragoons to charge the collapsing French columns, but the charge continued too far without proper control and many riders and horses were lost.

The mass of Sir Arthur's men remained behind the crest of the ridge north of Vimeiro out of the way of French fire, until they advanced and drove the French away to the north. Another French column was driven back just before noon, and the British won the day. Sir Arthur is said to have ridden up to

Copy of the draft of the Convention of Cintra. Following defeat at Vimeiro the French discovered themselves to be almost cut off from retreat and entered negotiations, which were agreed at Cintra (or Sintra), Estramadura. The terms were generous, allowing the French to depart with their guns and booty onboard British ships. Wellesley claimed to have signed under orders from his commanding officer, leading to a storm of protest in Britain.
The British Library, Add. MS.49484, f.60

This is the City of Lisbon.

This is the Gold, that lay in the City of Lisbon.

These are the French who took the [Gold] that lay in the City of Lisbon.

This is the Convention that Nobody owns, that saved old Junots Baggage and Bones, altho Sir Arthur (whose Valour and skill began so well but ended so ill,) had beaten the French who took the Gold that lay in the City of Lisbon.

These are the Ships that carried the spoil, that the French had plundered much foil, after the convention which, nobody owns, that saved Old Junots and Bones, altho Sir Arthur (whose Valour & skill began so well but ended so had beaten the French who took the Gold, that lay in the City of Lisbon.

Woodward del.

THE CONVENTION of CINTRA, a Portuguese Gambol for the

Sir Harry, raised his hat, and told him, 'Sir Harry, now is your time to advance. The enemy are completely beaten, we shall be in Lisbon in three days.' Sir Harry answered: 'Wait for Moore.' The army would not advance without support. Sir Arthur told his officers that they might as well go hunting.

On 22 August, Junot proposed a negotiated surrender, sending General François-Etienne Kellermann to discuss terms. The proposals were read to Sir Arthur, and then drafted by Kellermann and Sir Hew Dalrymple, who had arrived to take command. Kellermann suggested that Sir Arthur, who was of an equal rank to him, should sign it. Sir Arthur obliged. The armistice was then converted into a formal convention at Cintra, in the hills above Lisbon. The

Sir Arthur(whose Valour and skill,
so well, but ended so ill) who beat the
who took the Gold, that lay in the
Lisbon.

John Bull, in great dismay, at the sight
ships, which carried away, the gold and
d all the spoil, the French had plundered
uch toil, after the convention which nobody
ich saved old Junot's Baggage and Bones
Arthur (whose Valour and Skill, began
t ended so ill) had, unless the French
the Gold, that lay in the City of Lisbon.

on Publ. Feb. 3. 1809 by Thos. Tegg 111 Cheapside.
nt of IOHN BULL.
3 Feb. 1809

The Convention of Cintra, 1809, engraving by Woodward. The decision to allow the French army to leave in British boats with their arms and looted gold was widely deplored in Britain.
The British Museum, 11215

French were to leave Portugal, but were free to take their captured treasure and were to be shipped home in British vessels. Although the British expedition force's position had been stretched, they had won a brilliant victory at Vimeiro, and the terms of the convention, although sensible, were seen almost as treason by many in Britain.

Sir Arthur, no longer needed in Portugal (and declining the offer of staying to survey northern Spain), returned to London. It was not a happy homecoming. His marriage with Kitty was under strain and the family had to weather the twin scandals of Richard's philandering and the elopement of Sir Arthur's sister-in-law Lady Charlotte Wellesley with Henry, Lord Paget, his former commander of cavalry. Richard was also under attack for his warmongering and use of public money in India, and Sir Arthur's own involvement with the Convention of Cintra brought public odium. A military inquiry began on 14 November in the Great Hall of Chelsea College (it is now Chelsea Hospital). In December, the court approved the Convention by six votes to one and accepted its details by four to three. Burrard and Dalrymple never commanded again, and Sir Arthur could claim that he had no choice but to sign out of duty; this was something less than the truth, and Sir Arthur could count on political allies to extricate him from blame.

Meanwhile, disturbed by the news from the Iberian peninsula, Napoleon himself had taken command of the army in Spain. He quickly recaptured Madrid and drove out the new British Commander-in-Chief, Sir John Moore, who managed to rescue Cadiz and Lisbon before he was killed at Coruña in January

1809. Napoleon handed the command on to Marshal Jean-de-Dieu Soult, a brilliant French officer who had risen from the ranks. Soult was soon in Oporto. In Britain, support for the war had crumbled, and the Whigs and radicals openly attacked the Iberian policy. Sir Arthur continued to lobby for continued British support of the Spanish and Portuguese. Castlereagh was convinced and began to persuade the cabinet; on 22 April, Sir Arthur arrived in Lisbon, finding the city in celebration in his honour. This next campaign was to differ from the template of British operations, which relied on the close support of the British navy; as a contemporary soldier noted, 'a landing, a short march, and a good fight, and then a lounge home again'. The Iberian expedition was to be a war of attrition, with marches deep inland, a reliance on extensive lines of supply and the need to carefully conserve the numbers of his men. Sir Arthur had also seen the harshness of the land and the complexities of working alongside his Spanish and Portuguese allies. Thirty years later, he recalled that he never worried about victory, 'but it was the daily detail that was the weight upon me. I never walked out, or rode out, or took a moment's recreation without having some affair or other occupying my thoughts.'

Making careful preparations – gathering bullocks, carts and other supplies – Sir Arthur planned to attack Soult in northern Portugal, then undertake a combined Anglo-Spanish operation against the French in central Spain. He commandeered all the boats he could muster to prevent the French crossing the Tagus into Portugal from Spain, and marched north, surprising the French on 12 May at Oporto, where they were expecting an amphibious attack and at first mistook the British for Swiss soldiers fighting for the French. Soult retreated north, abandoning his gold, guns and wounded to the Portuguese. It was time to turn to Spain.

In Britain, Sir Arthur was accused of failing to chase Soult with enough vigour, that he was only intending to defend Portugal and that his position was precarious. His political enemies, many of whom wished for peace with Napoleon, also caused trouble.

In Britain, Sir Arthur was accused of failing to chase Soult with enough vigour, that he was only intending to defend Portugal and that his position remained unduly precarious. His political enemies, many of whom wished for peace with Napoleon, also caused trouble. Yet he did face real problems: Soult had retreated out of reach, but the French superiority of numbers remained a potent threat; within Portugal, his troops' behaviour and looting threatened his relations with the Portuguese. To counter this, Sir Arthur instituted harsh, demonstrable discipline, such as public floggings, and the creation of a military police (modelled on the French system), aimed to deal with the British soldier's customary inclination towards drunken looting.

His next military operations were less successful, in part because of difficult relations with his Spanish allies. On 10 July, Sir Arthur was to meet with the aged Spanish general, Don Gregario de la Cuesta, near the Tagus bridge at Almaraz, but due to a lack of maps was five hours late. The two commanders planned to meet again on 21 July and march on the French forces under Marshal Claude Victor. By 23 July, Victor's 20,000 men had withdrawn in the face of the Anglo-Spanish and Portuguese force of 52,000; Sir Arthur planned to attack, but Cuesta complained that his troops were too tired and they should attack the next day. That night, Victor withdrew again, and the opportunity to strike had passed.

Unbeknown to the allies, Victor had joined forces with the French troops under General Horace Sebastiani and Napoleon's brother King Joseph, forming a force of some 46,000, and the armies bumped into one another. Sir Arthur persuaded Cuesta to withdraw his troops to a defensive position at Talavera on the bank of the Tagus. As he oversaw the deployment of the British and Portuguese troops from the top of a tall farmhouse he was surprised by a party of French skirmishers at the base of the building, narrowly escaping on horseback. Sporadic fighting continued through the night of 27 July, during which some 2,000 Spanish troops fled. The battle proper began early the next day, when the British and Portuguese army of 20,000 faced 40,000 French (the Spanish formed a defensive block to the south). The French attacked three times before a truce at around 11 a.m., when troops from both sides drank from the Portina stream in the heat of the Spanish sun. After noon, the French unleashed two great assaults on the centre of the British line. The French were beaten back by close-range volleys of musket fire. The final French attack sent forward over 10,000 experienced troops, and the British appeared to be about to collapse. Sir Arthur saw that a Guards brigade and two brigades of the King's German Legion had advanced too far and had been cut to shreds, leaving a gap in the British line; seeing the danger, he immediately ordered 3,000 men to fill the gap and the French advance was repelled. By the next morning, the French had gone. 'Never was there such a Murderous Battle', Sir Arthur noted; fire had broken out on the following afternoon, killing many of the wounded and leaving a blackened sea of charred bodies and horses. The carnage, he thought, was even worse than Assaye, and was 'two days of the hardest fighting I have ever been party too'. He wrote to the Duke of Richmond, 'You will see the account of the great battle we fought yesterday. Our loss is terribly great ... Almost all my staff are hurt or have lost their horses, and how I have escaped unhurt I cannot tell. I was hit in the shoulder at the end of the action, but not hurt, and my coat shot through.'

Although an unquestioned victory, Talavera did not pave the way to Madrid. Instead, Sir Arthur was forced to operate defensively: the British had lost a quarter of their men and, within a day, the Allies received the unwelcome news that Marshal Soult was preparing to advance with fresh, well-trained troops; they also faced six other French corps. Soult threatened the British supply lines and

'Never was there such a Murderous Battle', Sir Arthur noted; fire had broken out on the following afternoon, killing many of the wounded and leaving a blackened sea of charred bodies and horses.

The Iberian campaign, 1808–1814, showing the main British engagements.

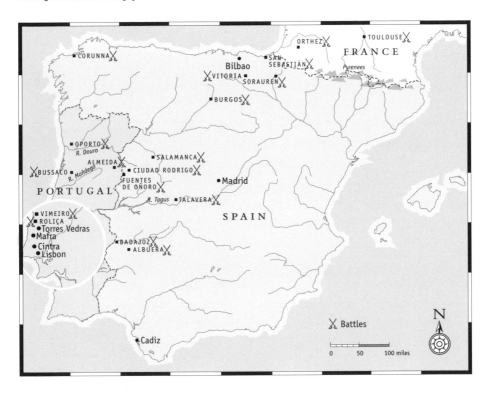

the Spanish were defeated twice in September. Sir Arthur's brother Lord Wellesley had arrived as ambassador to the Spanish junta, and was quickly warned of the need for new supplies, since 'a starving army is worse than none'. Sir Arthur also faced political opposition from Britain when now he decided to retreat to Portugal. Lord Portland's administration, which included Sir Arthur's political ally Lord Castlereagh, had fallen following the total defeat of a British expedition to the Dutch island of Walcheren in the Scheldt (Castlereagh and George Canning fought a duel on Putney Heath over the handling of the matter), and the opposition were calling for retreat from Portugal. The two Wellesleys had to persuade the new government, led by Spencer Perceval, that Portugal could be held. Lord Wellesley returned to become Foreign Secretary. Sir Arthur sought to improve the behaviour of his troops and silence the 'croakers' (as he dubbed complaining officers) while secretly working on his plans for the defence of Portugal from the French onslaught. He could at least take some enjoyment from his elevation to the peerage as a viscount: after 'ransacking the Peerage and examining the map', his brother William settled on 'Wellington', a town to the west of Wells, Somerset. Sir Arthur signed himself 'Wellington' for the first time on 16 September 1809.

In the autumn and winter of 1809–10, Wellington prepared for the defence of Portugal, making use of the harsh environment and the Portuguese tradition of a scorched-earth defence against invaders (which also caused enormous suffering for the peasantry). Under Wellington and his surveyor Fletcher's detailed instructions, the Portuguese and British built three lines of defence between the Tagus and the sea. A network of forts with trenches and ramparts running between them, damned rivers and broken roads posed a severe obstacle to any invading army. The defensive works became known as the 'Lines of Torres Vedras' after the town through which the longest line, of twenty-nine miles, ran. The effort taken in their construction was massive. The forts and lines were manned by 25,000 Portuguese militia, 8,000 Spaniards and 2,500 British marines and gunners, enabling the British, who had also incorporated Portuguese battalions in their ranks, to muster wherever the French decided to attack.

As expected, the French arrived in the spring of 1810. Napoleon had ordered Marshal André Massena's 138,000 men to throw the British into the sea. Massena began to take control of the strategic points on the northern routes into Portugal, first capturing the Spanish fortress of Cuidad Rodrigo on 10 July and then the Portuguese fortress of Almeida on 28 August. The French then advanced south with a force of around 50,000 men. Wellington met them with a similar-sized force on 27 September at Bussaco, a village on a ridge running across the Mondego valley. The French lost 4,500 men to Wellington's 1,252, but continued their advance in the inhospitable countryside, which had been razed in advance. Wellington wrote, 'My opinion is that the French are in a scrape.' He withdrew behind the lines of Torres Vedras on 8 October, and the French, after losing 500 men a week through sickness, hunger and attacks by the Portuguese, retreated to the north-west in March 1811. The lines of Torres Vedras had held.

The campaign then became a matter of protracted sieges and counter-thrusts by the opposing sides, with Wellington attempting to orchestrate two fronts. Wellington sent General Beresford to besiege the French-held border fortress of Badajoz, while he moved north. The French counter-attacked both advances, at Fuentes de Oñoro – where Wellington defeated Massena at the cost of 2,000 men – and at Almeida, where Beresford narrowly defeated Soult, losing 6,000 men. Wellington galloped to join Beresford when he heard that Soult was attacking (two horses died under him on the ride), but he arrived too late. He realized that the British could not sustain such losses, and after failing to storm either Badajoz or Fort San Cristóbal, moved north to lay siege to Ciudad Rodrigo. By January 1812, the French numbers were depleted by the need to help Marshal Louis Suchet's battles with the Spanish, and Wellington was reinforced by Major General Sir Rowland Hill's troops and siege guns. On 19 January, after a freezing, bloody winter, the walls of Ciudad Rodrigo were breached by the British. Although the French managed to explode a mine under the Light Division as they assaulted the fortress with its brilliant, stubborn commander, Robert Crauford, at the head of the charge, they saw that they were finally defeated and surrendered. The British troops then ransacked the town in an orgy of looting. A few days later, Crauford died from his wounds, with Wellington at his side observing that 'he talked to me as they do in a novel'.

Next, Wellington attacked Badajoz, a far more formidable fortress than Ciudad Rodrigo: as he wrote following the siege, 'a most serious undertaking ... the assault was a terrible business, of which I saw the loss when I ordered it'. The French repelled more than forty attacks, until finally Lieutenant MacPherson, suffering from two broken ribs, tore down the French flag and replaced it with his red jacket, while Sir James Leith and Sir Thomas Picton led two other charges. The Allies lost some 5,000 men. Again, the capture of the town led to mass drunkenness and looting by the British troops. After two days, Wellington ordered the plunder to cease, erected a gallows as a warning in the central square, and began to repair the fortress's defences.

Meanwhile, he sent out a series of diversionary movements to distract the French, before heading to Salamanca. He arrived on 17 June 1812, and began to manoeuvre against the French under General Auguste Marmont. On the morning of 22 July, it became clear that the two armies – of around 50,000 apiece – would clash on the great plain of Salamanca. Wellington chose his ground with great care to conceal his troops, manoeuvred his forces with brilliance and attacked with vigour. At around midday, he saw that the French were still moving to the west, exclaimed, 'By God, that will do,' and, not trusting anyone else to deliver his orders, galloped out to the lines. He threw Edward Pakenham's 3rd Division at the French in a column, asking his brother-in-law to

Chalk sketch of Lord Wellington by
Francisco Goya, made soon after
Wellington entered Madrid following
the Battle of Salamanca in 1812.
The British Museum, 1862-7-12-185

'drive them to the devil'. As Pakenham's division met the French, Wellington unleashed a series of devastating attacks on the spread-out French flanks, including a heavy cavalry charge under Lieutenant General Sir Stapleton Cotton that led him to exclaim, 'By God, Cotton, I never saw anything more beautiful in my life. The day is yours.' Marmont lost 14,000 men and twenty guns, to the Allies' 7,000. News of the French defeat reached Napoleon on the eve of the Battle of Borodino, where the Emperor would fail to crush the Russian army. The Prince Regent rewarded Wellington for Salamanca with a marquessate, and a grateful parliament voted him £100,000 towards a victor's mansion.

Wellington himself was exhausted, and contemporary portraits such as that by Goya show his wearied eyes. His men continued to trouble their Spanish hosts and went for months without pay. Like his men, he had suffered through the cold and damp of winter in the Iberian hills and in the heat and dry of the summer. He maintained a punishing schedule, sleeping in his clothes, often eating only cold bread and meat, taking minute care with every detail of planning and operations, producing voluminous correspondence and overseeing as much as possible in person. He managed to maintain his energy through catnaps, having the ability to sleep wherever he found himself. Once, exhausted before a battle, and with nothing more to do, he once simply lay down, placed a newspaper over his eyes and requested to be woken when the French arrived. His office and quarters was a pavilion, with a smaller tent erected inside with a small steel-framed bed. His cook prepared food from a tarpaulin-covered trench outside. Relaxation could be found in foxhunting, balls and possibly in the arms of women, such as the Spanish lady who left what Elizabeth Longford terms in her biography, a 'brief but affectionate' letter among his papers.

That autumn, Wellington also suffered the shock of the death of Major the

Hon. Edward Somers Cocks,
who died of a musket shot
during an assault on the fortified
town of Burgos. Somers had
been a favourite among the
able, young and aristocratic men
with whom Wellington liked to
surround himself, expecting them
to undertake reconnaissance
work and delivered high-level
communications. When he heard
of the death, he went to the
room of one of his staff and
announced, 'Cocks was killed
last night,' but could say nothing
more. No one dared to speak to
him at the funeral. It was one
death among many, but shows
that even Wellington's famed
emotional reserve could be

broached. On another occasion, he was observed emerging from visiting Lord
March, who had been badly wounded, in tears.

The army failed to take Burgos, and retreated in the face of French troops
and terrible weather; his men were also waylaid by the wine-harvest: Wellington
thought it 'the worst scrape I ever was in'. The victory at Salamanca had almost
been squandered. Furthermore, he insulted his officers by complaining in a

Previous pages: Wellington bivouacking
in the Pyrenees, from Edward Orme,
Historic, Military, and Naval Anecdotes,
1819. He lived frugally on campaigns,
and when asked what time the staff
should leave in the morning would
invariably reply 'At daylight.
Cold meat.'
The British Library, J.9080.m.3

general order of the 'habitual inattention of the officers of the regiments to their
duty'. The order found its way to England, and was printed in the newspapers as
an addition to the growing complaints at what became known as the 'mad
Marquess's' behaviour in Spain. He remained in Portugal for the winter, preparing
his troops and his plans.

On 22 May 1813, the army returned to Spain. Wellington supposedly turned,
doffed his hat and announced: 'Farewell, Portugal! I shall never see you again.'
He knew that the French were weakened. Napoleon's Grande Armée had been
destroyed in the retreat from Moscow, and Spanish forces had been harassing the
French in Spain. Joseph had given up Madrid and was marching north in an
attempt to join forces with the French forces under General Bertrand Clausel.
In a brilliantly planned advance, Wellington marched past Burgos, watching as the
French exploded it instead of making a stand, and then, on 21 June, met them at
Vitoria. Wellington sent two columns from the west as the French were expecting,
and then attacked from the north as the French were pinned down. In the ensuing
rout, the French lost all their baggage and the majority of their guns. Wellington's
reputation was restored. Beethoven composed 'Wellington's Victory' in its honour,
and the Prince Regent appointed him Field Marshal for his 'glorious conduct'.

But again, the victory was undermined by British looting and drunkenness
after the battle, which prevented the pursuit and destruction of the French.
'We may gain the greatest victories', Wellington argued in a letter, 'but we shall
do no good, until we shall so far alter our system, as to force all ranks to perform
their duty'. Still, France's hold on Spain had been broken, and the French were
now merely trying to hold the Pyrenees. Soult replaced King Joseph in July,
regrouped his forces and counter-attacked. He defeated small contingents of the
British at Roncesvalles and Maya, but Wellington halted him at Sorauren at the

end of July, escaping 'unhurt as usual … I begin to believe that the finger of God is upon me'.

Providence did not favour an attack on the fortress at San Sebastián, which took almost three months to fall, and then succumbed to flames and British pillaging. The Allied advance to the north-east coast of Spain was held back by Marshal Suchet, but Wellington received news that Napoleon was suffering in Germany and decided to take the passes of the Pyrenees. He broke the French defences at Vera, and then, with the Spanish, brushed aside resistance on the Nivelle, the Nive and at St Pierre, moving through France towards Toulouse. Soult's forces were beaten at Orthez on 27 February 1814, where Wellington was wounded in the thigh by a musket ball. Luckily, his sword-hilt broke the force, but he was left with a limp for several days.

Once in France, Wellington could no longer rely on a network of sympathizers for information, which had served him well in Spain, and he was unsure of Soult's movements. Rumours of Napoleon's success in holding back the Russians, Prussians and Austrians also reached him. He considered it prudent to take Toulouse, which was believed to be a royalist city. Soult retreated ahead of him, and on 12 April Wellington rode into the red-stone French city, finding Napoleon's statue smashed. As he prepared for an official dinner, the news of the Emperor's abdication reached Wellington: 'Ay, 'tis time indeed. You don't say so, upon my honour! Hurrah!' he answered the messenger, clicking his fingers like a flamenco dancer. That evening, he was toasted and cheered as the liberator of Spain. Clearly embarrassed, he bowed and called for coffee.

Napoleon later wrote that it was the Spanish war 'that overthrew me. All my disasters can be traced back to this fatal knot'. Most British historians have happily agreed with this view, arguing that British involvement in the peninsula gave vital support to the Spanish army and guerrilla movement, draining crucial resources from Napoleon's attack on Russia in 1812 and his defence of France in 1813 and 1814. Even more damaging to Napoleon was the destruction of his aura of invincibility; as Portugal and Spain expelled the French, so opposition to his regime in France and Europe grew, and Austria and Russia gained the courage to attack. Yet this view is something of a distortion; undoubtedly, Napoleon's opponents drew succour from his Iberian troubles, but Napoleon was defeated not by his lack of troops in Russia, but by the Russian winter and the Grand Armée's inadequate logistical support. Russia then drew Prussia and Austria into the war on her behalf. As a British historian of the Peninsular War, Charles Esdaile, has commented, 'Napoleon fell not because the Peninsular War had any influence on Russian, Prussian or Austrian policy, but because it failed to have any influence on French policy.'

The consequences for Portugal and Spain, however, were far ranging. Both countries' economies were effectively destroyed, along with much of their overseas empires, famine and disease dramatically reduced life expectancy, their armies became politicized and civil war dominated political life for the next generation and beyond. Relations between Portugal, Spain and Britain were also severely taxed by suspicions of British adventurism. The adventure was, however, the making of Wellington. He carefully conserved his small number of troops, operating defensively, without missing decisive assaults at the right moment. His attention to detail ensured that the British army reached perhaps the highest point of effectiveness for generations: to take just one example, he gave orders to replace cast-iron camp kettles with lighter tin ones, so that the pack mules could carry tents for the cold and damp mountain conditions. He displayed a cool unflappability in the face of danger, dissent from his officers and political

opposition in Britain; nor did he take a day of leave from April 1809 to April
1814 (although he found time for hunting). Furthermore, despite his disdain for
the Spanish forces, he managed to operate with them and gave support to the
guerrilla movement. There were errors – for example, the mishandling of siege
warfare – but the campaign stands as one of the most brilliant – and gruelling –
of British military expeditions.

3

... at the age of forty-five,
Wellington accepted the position
of Ambassador to France.

A desperate business

Wellington did not return to Britain immediately. His brothers had fallen out of favour with the Liverpool administration and, consequently, appointment to a British political post was unlikely. Instead, at the age of forty-five, Wellington accepted the position of Ambassador to France, as well as a dukedom. On 4 May, wearing civilian clothes – a blue cloak and top hat – rather than military uniform, he entered the city and caused an immediate sensation. The Paris crowd and high society were equally eager to catch a glimpse of the British soldier. He soon got down to official work and was called upon to visit Spain to oversee the restoration of King Ferdinand VII. Following a short season of balls, soirées and official business back in Paris, he returned to London on 23 June. Here, the crowds welcoming the military hero were immense; at Westminster Bridge the throng unhitched his carriage's horses, intending to pull him to his home at 4 Hamilton Place. Wellington's response to this display was to take a horse and leave the mob to it, riding ahead to Kitty and his two sons, whom he had not seen for five years. He stayed at his house only a matter of hours before escaping to call on his mother. He then endured a whirl of official banquets, toasts and celebrations.

In August, he returned to Paris, travelling via the Netherlands and what is now Belgium. He later claimed that he noted the 'good positions for an army' provided by the 'entrance to the forêt de Soignes by the high road which leads to Brussels' – the ground on which he would fight Napoleon at the Battle of Waterloo the following year. He arrived in Paris on 22 August – with Kitty following him that autumn – and moved into his official residence at 39 rue du Faubourg-St-Honoré, which had been owned by Napoleon's younger sister and remains the British Embassy today. The task facing him was considerable. France had been devastated by years of war, had lost almost three-quarters of a million men and was suffering from economic dislocation. The political position was also

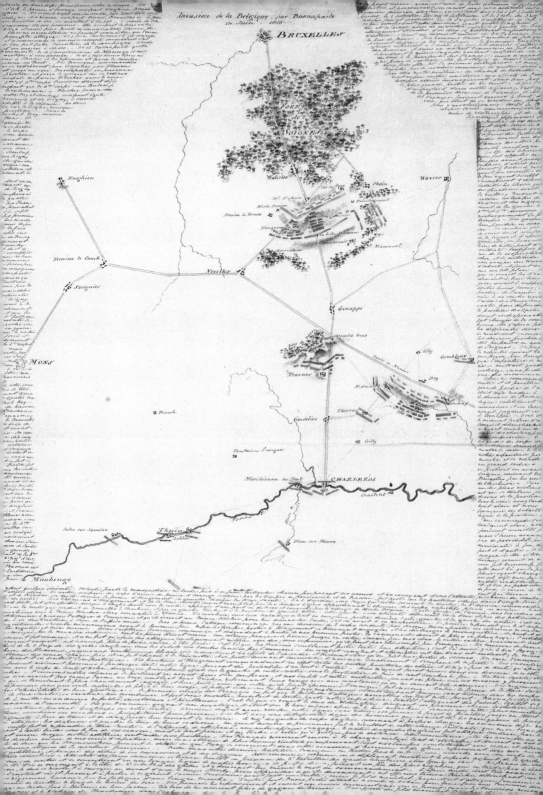

tense, since the conquering powers had reinstated the French monarchy in the corpulent figure of Louis XVIII, while many French still supported Napoleon or remained moderate monarchists or republicans, and distrusted the influence of returning émigrés surrounding Louis. The question of how to constrain France's power and what to do with the former emperor also confronted the Allies.

At this time, Wellington also met several of his former opponents, including Soult and Massena. The latter approached Wellington with the words, 'My lord, you owe me a dinner – for you positively made me starve.' The Duke replied: 'You should give it to me, for you prevented me from sleeping.' Wellington never met Napoleon, but did meet the opera singer Josephina Grassini and the actress Marguerite Josephine Weimer, both of whom had been the Emperor's mistresses. Wellington probably took them on in this capacity as well, and, Weimer claimed, with more success. Harriette Wilson also claimed to have had a liaison with the Duke in the Bois de Boulogne. He met his match in Madame de Staël, the French author and hostess, with whom he struck up a lasting, if intellectually antagonistic, friendship.

Although fêted socially, Wellington had become a hate-figure in the French press. Louis XVIII's grip on power was weak, and the British feared a coup by the French army. The British government feared for Wellington's life and sought to find the Duke an alternative posting, despite his protests that 'I don't like to be frightened away'. Commander-in-Chief of North America was considered, but Vienna, where the congress of European powers was taking place, was decided upon. As Austrian agents rifled through the wastepaper baskets, the future map of Europe was slowly being redrawn. Wellington threw himself into the negotiations, which he regarded as having become interminably mired; with Kitty still in Paris, he also found the brilliant Viennese social life to be highly congenial.

Souvenir of Napoleon

...s used as a poster for the play of

...gal Divorce. The Rev James White in his History

...ing to the expected return of Napoleon from Elba says,

...were whispers about great things that would occur ...

Conu fecit

Violettes
du 20 Mars 1815.

déposée a la Direction generale   A Paris, rue St Jacques N° 29

BRITISH MUSEUM

...appeared in Spring. Ladies wore violets in their bonnets.

...Sketches were circulated in which the figure of a violet ...

...d that the interval between the leaves formed the well kn...

...nance of the Emperor with his plain grey riding coat & tri...

...he was talked of as Corporal Violet. If the description

Then, on 7 March 1815, just as Wellington was preparing to go out hunting (a favourite pursuit), the news of Napoleon's escape from his Mediterranean island prison of Elba reached Vienna. It soon became clear that as Napoleon travelled from Fréjus, on the south coast of France, to Paris he had gathered support and recreated an army. In response, the Allies began to marshal three armies: Austrian troops in northern Italy, a combined force in the upper Rhine and a predominately Prussian force in the lower Rhine which would join British and Hanoverian troops in the Netherlands. In Poland, the mass of the Russian army formed a reserve. But although the Allies had a numerical advantage on paper, they feared that Napoleon would succeed in striking and defeating the individual armies one by one, as he had almost succeeded in doing during his brilliant but doomed defence of France in 1814. Napoleon could then sue for peace and have his claim to the throne recognized.

Wellington could have remained as British ambassador in Vienna, but chose instead what he termed the 'musket': the command of the British troops in the Netherlands, where Napoleon was likely to strike first. Tsar Alexander sent him on his way with the words: 'It is for you to save the world again.'

Wellington normally rode hard, and he speedily arrived in Brussels from Vienna on 4 April after a six-day ride. He quickly set about improving the troops that he had to hand, who lacked experience and leadership. Few of his Peninsular officers were available: his brother-in-law and favourite, Edward Pakenham, had been killed in the American War of 1812, to his and Kitty's great distress; his trusted quartermaster was in Canada and was replaced by Sir Hudson Lowe ('a damned fool', thought Wellington); while the able cavalry commander Sir Stapleton Cotton was superseded by Lord Uxbridge. Wellington could still count on Sir Thomas Picton, 'a rough foul-mouthed devil', but one that 'no man

Many of his Peninsular regiments were in North America, and many of the British were new recruits, who could not necessarily be relied upon to withstand the crashing impact of veteran French columns.

could do better'. Many of his Peninsular regiments were in North America, and many of the British were new recruits, who could not necessarily be relied upon to withstand the crashing impact of veteran French columns. The majority of Wellington's troops were Hanoverians who, the British assumed, lacked the training of their English, Scottish, Welsh or Irish counterparts. He made the best use of his Peninsular veterans that he could, dispersing them among the new men and combining British and Hanoverian units; in the military historian Richard Holme's phrase, 'laminating' the new multinational army.

As ever, Wellington was fighting expeditionary warfare with a limited number of troops. These factors drove his military strategy. As in India and the Peninsula, he had to defend crucial lines of supply and conserve his men; he was aware that he could not unduly risk the bulk of Britain's army, particularly with political unrest increasing in Britain and Ireland. In addition, as an expeditionary force, the British needed to defend access to their North Sea ports; at all costs, Wellington had to avoid being cut off from these routes, and he saw that the defence of Brussels was the key to his position. Belgium, which had been French for twenty years, was also a likely target for early annexation by Napoleon. As during the Peninsular campaigns, Wellington also had to work with other nations, now liaising with King William I of the Netherlands and the Prince of Orange, whom the King had superseded as Commander-in-Chief until Wellington took overall command. Relations with King William took some time to improve after a cool start.

Wellington split the army into three corps, the first commanded by the Prince of Orange, the second consisting of two British and two Hanoverian divisions led by Lord Hill and the third – the reserves – commanded by Wellington himself, with a corps under the Duke of Brunswick. In all, Wellington

Map of the Battle of Waterloo, after
1815. Wellington made brilliant use
of the ground to defend the route
to Brussels.
The British Library, Add. MS. 57653, f.2

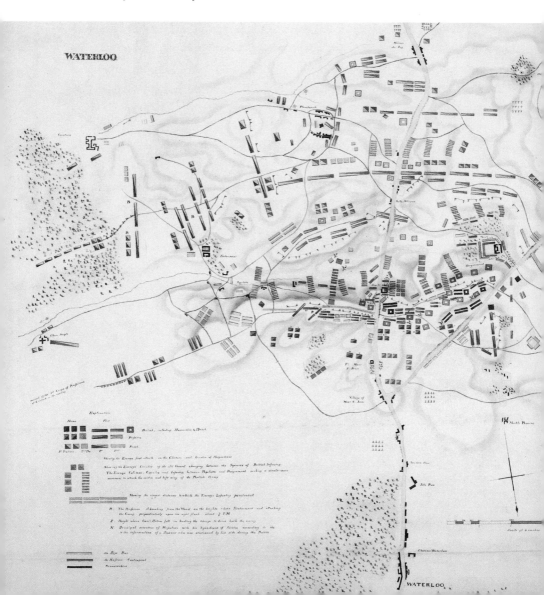

controlled 92,000 men and 192 guns. Most importantly, Wellington had to cooperate with the 121,000-strong Prussian army, commanded by the eccentric seventy-two-year-old General Gebhard von Blücher, Prince of Wahlstadt. Wellington and Blücher had met previously at Paris in 1814, and got along well. Now, Allied victory depended on effective cooperation between the two men and their armies. The clash with Napoleon was to be a resolutely international affair.

Thanks to his intelligence network, Wellington knew that Napoleon had raised some 124,000 men. The former artillery officer could also call on 344 guns, far more than Wellington. The central core of this army was the proudly bewhiskered Imperial Guard, itself divided into the Old and Young Guard. The French army was divided into five further corps. The capable Marshal Soult, Wellington's foe from the Spanish campaign, acted as Napoleon's chief of staff. But the new army faced similar problems to that commanded by Wellington: new recruits mixed uneasily with veterans, and not all troops preferred Napoleon to the Bourbons. Furthermore, Soult lacked the tactical ability of some of Napoleon's former commanders, not all of whom had returned to him after his escape from Elba.

The state of Napoleon's health during the campaign continues to be a matter for debate. Anglophone historians have often concluded that he was in rude form, while French or pro-Napoleon historians have pointed to the debilitating after-effects of an attempted poisoning, tumours on the pituitary glands, bladder infections or the flu. Most of these medical diagnoses can be seen as attempts to explain away an unexpected defeat for a master general rather than substantive claims, but it seems fair to see Napoleon as lacking something of his former energy on the night before and the day of the Battle of Waterloo. At the very least, his haemorrhoids made riding uncomfortable – a clear disadvantage in someone who had to oversee a battle on a vast scale.

Despite any real or imaginary medical problems, Napoleon's opening moves were as brilliant as any in his military career. In June, after mustering his army in a miraculously short period, he rapidly advanced through modern-day Belgium, leaving the Allies wholly uncertain about his exact movements. There were three likely routes for a French attack, and Wellington deployed his forces to meet any of them; this meant that his troops were dangerously dispersed and had to be prepared to muster wherever the French attacked. But Napoleon had discovered what Wellington feared most: he had found the 'hinge' between Wellington's and Blücher's armies, through which he could then defeat one army at a time, or push on to Brussels, cutting the Allies off from supplies. Following this victory, the French could then turn to the Austrians in the south or sue for peace before the steamroller of the Russian army arrived.

Wellington's response to Napoleon's advance has continued to vex historians of the campaign. British historians have tended to assert that Wellington's intelligence operations were severely hampered by Napoleon's feints and the closure of the French borders; Wellington himself later suggested that the French attack took him by surprise – he was expecting Napoleon to attempt to cut his communications with the North Sea ports, a strategy of envelopment that Napoleon often used to devastating effect. This approach would have driven the British and Prussians together, but Wellington still considered it to be Napoleon's most likely strategy. Wellington's *Selected Dispatches* suggest that by the evening of 15 June at least, the British high command was well appraised of the French

The famous ball given by the Duchess of Richmond on the eve of battle, where, as Byron had it, 'The lamps shone o'er fair women and brave men', took place in a converted coachbuilder's workshop on 15 June.

position and that a flow of fairly accurate intelligence had reached Wellington for several weeks. Some historians, such as Peter Hofschröer, have suggested that Wellington either deceived his allies or made a mistake and attempted to cover up his failings after the event. As was his wont, Wellington discussed his overall strategy with no one and his plans remain a matter of conjecture. At root, he believed that Napoleon was an opportunist, who would adapt to circumstances. Wellington believed that he must remain cautious and responsive, ensuring, as he later remarked, that he made no 'false Movement'. With this in mind, the army waited through spring, dispersed across the Netherlands. Key points, such as Mons, were defended, and Wellington worked diligently on his administration.

The waiting game provided time for other activities. Wellington was based in Brussels, with the responsibility for the safety of the royal family. The city was crowded by a great number of British visitors, including Wellington's mother (he advised her to depart for Antwerp). Lady Frances Wedderburn-Webster, one of Lord Byron's devotees, soon became a close friend and the two were spotted walking together in the woods. Discreet gossip soon spread. The famous ball given by the Duchess of Richmond on the eve of battle, where, as Byron had it, 'The lamps shone o'er fair women and brave men', took place in a converted coachbuilder's workshop on 15 June. The Duchess is recorded as saying in May that she did 'not wish to pry into' Wellington's 'secrets', but she asked whether she might give her ball. 'Duchess,' he replied, 'you may give your ball with the greatest of safety, without fear of interruption', although he later warned her off giving a picnic near the French border. The Duke himself was planning to give a ball on 21 June, the anniversary of the Battle of Vitoria, suggesting that he did not then think that the campaign would begin until July. Although he had received news of the French advance on the route through Charleroi, he had made his

Map showing key locations during the
Battle of Waterloo, June 1815.

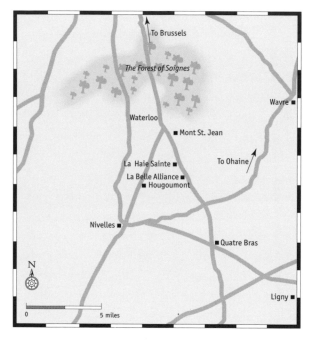

preparations and to cancel the ball would only be to create panic in the potentially rebellious city of Brussels. Furthermore, orders could be distributed at the ball.

The extent of Wellington's knowledge of Napoleon's movements at this point and the timing of the arrival of messengers remains controversial; some have suggested that Wellington was taken by surprise, or even suppressed information to make good his mistake. As far as can be seen, the balance of evidence supports Wellington's version of events. By 10 p.m., Wellington still wondered whether the main assault would be on Mons to the west. He arrived at the ball around 10:30 p.m. and was, as ever, the centre of attention. Despite his typical show of sangfroid, close observers noted an inner anxiety. By midnight, the Prince of Orange had arrived, whispering news of the attack on Quatre Bras in Wellington's ear. Wellington retired, asking the Duke of Richmond if he had a good map. It was at this point the Duke supposedly announced: 'Napoleon has humbugged me, by God! He has gained twenty-four hours' march on me.' Napoleon had found the gap between

Field Marshal von Blücher, Prince of Wahlstadt. An experienced soldier, Blücher helped to lead the allied armies into France in 1813–14. His command of the Army of the Lower Rhine in 1815 was crucial for victory at Waterloo.
The British Library, Egerton MS. 3719, f.36

the British and the Prussians and was marching on Brussels. Allied troops mustered at Quatre Bras and Nivelles to the east.

On 16 June Wellington rose at 5:30 a.m., took care of some letters and rode out at about 7 a.m., reaching Quatre Bras, twenty-two miles to the south of Brussels, at around 10 a.m. The Netherlanders still commanded the crossroads and the French did not appear to be coming on. He then rode and met the Prussian commander, Blücher, at Bussy windmill, who confirmed that he would soon be attacked. The Prussian position looked weak: 'If they fight here, they will be damnably mauled,' Wellington confided. He agreed to send reinforcements in the afternoon, 'provided that I am not attacked'. He returned to Quatre Bras to find that he faced about 42,000 French under Marshal Ney with around 6,000 men. Already, French skirmishers were advancing under the support of the superior French artillery. But coming to Wellington's aid were Picton's men, marching under a hot June sun and with some of his officers still dressed in their silk stockings from the ball. The Brunswicks arrived, led by the Duke of Brunswick himself, in two cavalry charges. He was killed in the final attack, and Wellington was almost caught during the rebuff by French cavalry. Riding Copenhagen hard, he bolted towards a battalion of Highlanders, yelling, 'Ninety-second, lie down!' jumping into the square before they unleashed murderous volleys to beat back the French.

The pattern of French cavalry charges continued through the day, with artillery slowly thinning the Allied line and ammunition running short. By late afternoon, the arrival of a brigade of the 3rd British Division and a Hanoverian brigade bolstered a desperately close-run battle. Then the Prince of Orange – who could not see any cavalry at that time – ordered the recently arrived British brigade to manoeuvre into line. The French returned almost immediately, driving two battalions back into a wood. The remaining battalion that had formed into a square to resist the cavalry attacks came under intense artillery fire. The battle looked lost, when Cooke's 1st British Division arrived, standing firm against the wood. The 92nd (the Highlanders), who had been fighting all day, then charged two columns of French infantry and stormed the buildings around the road. As the sun set, the Allies had reclaimed the ground they had lost at the cost of some 4,000 casualties. Wellington had been riding hard all day, at great personal risk, attempting to hold the line. The Allies had kept their position, but had failed to support the Prussians, who had faced the bulk of Napoleon's forces at Ligny and after – in Wellington's words – 'a damned good licking' retreated to Wavre. Following a few hours' sleep, Wellington ordered his forces to retreat northwards, endeavouring to conceal the manoeuvre as much as possible, 'making the men move at first under hedges and so on' and screening them with cavalry, to a low ridge known as Mont Saint-Jean, some twenty miles to the west of Wavre. This was protected to the east by valleys and woods and could be protected to the south by the defence of farm buildings at Hougoumont and La Haie Sainte. Some three miles or so to the north, in front of the forest of Soignes, lay the village of Waterloo.

By 3 p.m., Wellington received confirmation of Prussian support, but also discovered that a French force had been sent to intercept the Prussian march. He also heard that Blücher had almost been killed, only escaping from the French because he fell under his horse. The Prussian was attempting to revive his battered body in a bath of brandy. By nightfall, Wellington's troops had been put in place. Hougoumont was defended by a force of 1,500, made up of Foot Guards and German riflemen. Riflemen also garrisoned La Haie Sainte and took positions in a small pit to its front. Still suspecting a flanking movement, Wellington

Previous pages: Recruiting for the 33rd
Regiment, engraved by George Walker,
1814. Joining the army promised bread
as well as possible glory. Wellington
believed that the army recruited the
'scum of the earth' but turned them into
the 'fine fellows that they are'. Only
about a third of Wellington's army at
Waterloo were British.
The British Library, 143.g.1

dispatched a force of 15,000 to protect his western flank. The bulk of his forces were placed on the ridge's reverse slope in the Peninsular fashion, with his artillery forward.

The night contrasted with the heat of two days before, as the army shivered in the cold and rain under makeshift bivouacs made from muskets and blankets. Those who could warmed themselves with drink. The men who would fight what became known as the Battle of Waterloo came from across the United Kingdom – Scotland, England, Wales and Ireland – and from Hanover, Brunswick and the Netherlands. The Allies spoke four different languages. Wellington believed that he could count on the experienced strands of his army. The enemy were a similar mix of new and experienced troops, hastily formed into a new army, with commanders with differing abilities. Napoleon, however, remained a fear-inspiring enemy, who had recently marshalled an army and had brilliantly found the weak spot in the Allies' defence. He had defeated the Prussians at Ligny, and had dispatched a substantial force of 33,000 under Grouchy to distract the Prussians if they rallied and easily outnumbered Wellington's forces.

After a few hours' sleep at an inn at Waterloo, Wellington rose between 2 and 3 a.m., and immediately read and prepared his dispatches. Shortly after 7 a.m. he rode out on Copenhagen, wearing white breeches, a blue frock-coat and a black cocked hat. He wrapped himself in a blue cloak, as ever attempting to avoid getting damp and catching a chill. Accompanied by his staff, he rode around the positions, meeting with some friendly fire from some surprised Netherlander troops. He visited Hougoumont, where the gates had been burnt as firewood during the cold night, and returned to the centre of the army.

At 11 a.m. on 17 June, Napoleon launched a massive artillery bombardment and sent forward his troops in the traditional manner, a mass of columns attacking

Wellington's centre, following a diversionary attack on Hougoumont. The ground gave little room for manoeuvre, as did the relative inexperience of the troops, and the battle took place after the 'old style', with columns of men marching towards lines. Napoleon calculated that the Allies would be unable to withstand such a frontal assault and would retreat or flee. Wellington calculated that he could hold on until the Prussians arrived or retreat to the forest in his rear.

Napoleon's delay has caused controversy. Why did he not attack at dawn, ensuring victory long before the arrival of any potential Prussian reinforcements? The answer probably does not lie in any Napoleonic lethargy caused by ill-health or conspiracy, but in the state of the damp ground. Napoleon, the ex-artillery officer, had decided to let the ground dry somewhat to maximize the ricochet of his solid roundshot and allow his artillery pieces to be manoeuvred.

The emperor's youngest brother, Prince Jérôme, was at the head of the first attack of the day, on Hougoumont. Despite a howitzer bombardment, the French finally forced their way into the complex, but were driven out by a counter-charge and British artillery fire over the heads of the defenders. Wellington continued to keep the farm reinforced, drawing the French away from his centre. It remained in Allied hands throughout the day, at the cost of some 10,000 lives from both sides. Napoleon continued to pound the Allies' lines, although the carnage was lessened by the mud dampening the fall of shells and the protection of the ridge. At around 1:30 p.m. the French Marshal Comte d'Erlon's corps marched towards the Brussels road, arranged in line with two columns behind to combine strength with firepower. The Allies had saved their artillery ammunition and now fired at the advancing French with roundshot and then canister (musket balls in a tin case that fragmented on firing). Despite their losses, the French pushed back the Netherlands troops, but were held by British reinforcements.

La Belle Alliance, where Blücher and
Wellington met during the Battle of
Waterloo, by James Rouse. Blücher
proposed naming the battle after the inn.
The British Library, 193.e.9

Wellington recalled: 'They came on in the same old way, and we sent them back
in the same old way.'

Wellington had ridden to the west of the line and was overseeing the
defence of La Haie Sainte, under attack from French cavalry. He ordered his men
into a chequerboard of squares, and Lord Uxbridge ordered a cavalry charge at
the French infantry, who were run down. Although the cavalry captured two
eagles (the famous French regimental standards), they failed to regroup in time,
and lost too many horses and men to be used later in the day. Still, the Allied line

held. Wellington took care to be seen by his men, rallying their spirits, and rode
around the battle. The Allies then faced a massed cavalry charge, but this was
unsupported by infantry, and it was eventually rebuffed by their squares.

By 4:30 p.m., Wellington could hear the sound of cannon-fire from the east,
telling him that the Prussians were approaching. But the Allied line was severely
weakened: the squares in the centre were being worn down by continued cavalry
attacks and artillery fire, while Napoleon attempted to overwhelm the centre
through force of numbers. 'Damn the fellow,' exclaimed Wellington, about

Napoleon, 'he is a mere pounder after all'. La Haie Sainte, short of ammunition, was overrun at around 6:30 p.m., with only forty-three of its garrison escaping, and a mass of French infantry had been sent forward towards Wellington's critical centre. The Duke sent some reinforcements and with sustained volleys drove back the French. At last, at around 7 p.m., Napoleon sent forward his Guard, which had never been defeated, supported by the remains of d'Erlon's and General Honore Reille's troops. It was the crucial moment of the battle. Some 15,000 marched towards a ridge, behind which the 1st Foot Guards had been ordered to lie down. As the bearded and bear-skinned mass of Frenchmen approached, Wellington shouted 'Stand up, Guards!' and ordered the line to fire. The sustained volley from the front and side broke the attack. The battle had turned, and Wellington ordered his cavalry to advance. At 9 p.m., he met Blücher at the aptly named La Belle Alliance.

Wellington's men had no strength to pursue the French, and the Prussians took on this task (drummer-boys were tied to the Prussian cavalry in order to fool the exhausted French into believing that the enemy infantry was close on their heels). Napoleon himself was fleeing to Paris, where he could call on the National Guard of 70,000 men to defend the city. Wellington dined, toasting 'the Memory of the Peninsular War'. He was heard to say that 'the hand of almighty God has been upon me this day', and then quickly fell asleep.

The grim business of war soon returned. He was awoken by the arrival of the first casualty list. The British had suffered proportionally worse losses than they would at the Somme. Whole battalions, such as the 27th (Inniskilling) and the 73rd (Highland), had been almost destroyed. For many, the slaughter seemed worse than that at Assaye or Salamanca. The field was covered with mounds of dead: between 40,000 and 50,000 were killed or injured on the field. The

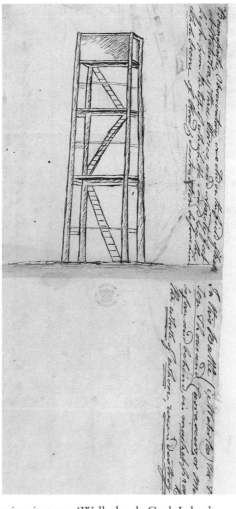

'Bounapartes [*sic*] Observatory erected on the field of Battle at Waterloo'. Several accounts and maps record a three-storey observatory built for Napoleon to oversee the battle, but there is no record of him making use of such a platform; more likely it was erected by the Prince of Orange. It was supposedly used by the many visitors to the battlefield. This sketch belonged to Sir W. H. Elliott, whose son fought at Waterloo.
The British Library, Add. MS. 42714, f.101b

Prussians and other Germans had also lost some 15,000 men. French casualties ran to 25,000. Almost half of the British officers had been killed or wounded, and Wellington was very nearly one of them – at some point in the afternoon grapeshot flew past him, hitting Lord Uxbridge in the knee, who announced, 'By God, sir, I've lost my leg'; Wellington looked down at his cavalry commander and replied simply, 'By God, sir, so you have.' Uxbridge's right leg would be amputated. After hearing Dr John Hume read to him the list of casualties, Wellington said, his face streaming in tears, 'Well, thank God, I don't know what it is to lose a battle; but certainly nothing can be more painful than to gain one with the loss of so many of one's friends.' That night, he woke at around three to the news that his friend William Gordon was dying. He later recalled that 'I went immediately to see him; but he was already dead.' At four in the morning, he rode to Brussels, since 'It was necessary to make new arrangements; so many officers were killed. We had to fill up the staff.'

The business of running an army also pressed him. The army had to be consolidated, reports had to be written, letters of consolation composed. Meanwhile, Napoleon could still call on 80,000 men. Wellington later told Lady

Shelley: 'While in the thick of it, I am too occupied to feel anything; but it is wretched just after. It is impossible to think of glory. Both mind and feelings are too exhausted.' He wrote to his brother William, 'It was the most desperate business I ever was in … and never was so near to being beat'. Waterloo was to be his last battle – at least on the field.

Napoleon had left Waterloo surrounded by a core of the Old Guard and sped back to Paris, where he arrived at the Elysée Palace at 5:30 p.m. on 21 June. He immediately ordered that Ney and Grouchy be reprimanded for disobeying orders, began to burn his state papers and laid the blame of his defeat on the desertion of the royalist General Louis Bourmont. Fearing a coup or civil war, Napoleon abdicated the next day in favour of the King of Rome, his son by the Austrian princess Marie-Louise, intending to continue as Commander-in-Chief of the Army. But his former Minister of Police, Joseph Fouché, led the Chambers in demanding that Napoleon leave Paris, and began to sue for peace. Wellington refused to accept while one of Napoleon's family was on the throne, answering Fouché: 'I continue my operation.' France finally capitulated on 3 July by the Convention of St-Cloud. Wellington denied Prussia's demands that Napoleon, who was awaiting arrest in Malmaison, be executed. On 1 July, the ex-Emperor had headed to the Atlantic coast, intending to find sanctuary in the Americas. On 8 July, the day that Louis XVIII re-entered Paris, Napoleon slipped out of Fouras on the French frigate *Saale*. The British government made it clear that Napoleon should be captured alive, but only if British seamen were not put at risk. Napoleon first attempted to secure a pass to the United States and then thought that he could seek asylum in Britain, drawing support from the pro-Napoleon Whigs and radicals; the idea horrified the Tory government. On 15 July, Napoleon boarded HMS *Bellerophon* and entered British custody, spending two weeks anchored in the

The Waterloo Despatch (detail). Wellington's draft of a message informing the Secretary of State for War of the victory over Napoleon. The despatch was composed over several hours, both at Waterloo and Brussels, as Wellington discovered more of the losses and victories of the day. 'I send with this despatch three eagles, taken by the troops in this action, which Major Percy will have the honour of laying at the feet of His Royal Highness. I beg leave to recommend him to your Lordship's protection.'
The British Library, Add. MS. 69850

Plymouth Sound. On 7 August Napoleon boarded HMS *Northumberland* to sail into exile on St Helena in the South Atlantic, the island that Wellington had found so healthful on his return from India a decade before.

The Duke returned to Paris as Commander-in-Chief of the Army of Occupation. Administration took up many of his waking hours; the Duke also continued 'to study by himself for some hours every day', as a friend noted. He argued for a sensible settlement, denying the Russians punitive reparations, and supported the centrist French politicians in the face of the more reactionary royalists. The Duke gave strict orders that his men were to respect their French hosts — for example, avoiding hunting on land without permission — and sought to rein in some of the Prussians' acts of revenge. Despite these efforts, he soon lost any favour he had with the French, when felt he could not interfere with the execution of Marshal Ney, the 'bravest of the brave', by the new government for treason.

The Duke also had to oversee the restoration of looted artworks that the Revolutionary and Napoleonic armies had gathered from across Europe. Many of them were on public display in the Louvre, and Louis XVIII felt that the policy of repatriation was an affront to his personal and national prestige. Wellington believed he was 'giving the people of France a moral lesson', that they could not hold on to the spoils from a war of 'national vanity'. He also argued against the French trade in black slaves, which had been reintroduced by the King following its re-abolition by Napoleon after his return from Elba. Too many of the King's circle stood to profit from the trade and Wellington failed.

In Britain, news of the victory gave birth to a Waterloo cult. News of the victory caused a sensation, but it was a mix of sadness and joy. Many read the casualty lists with keen attention, while others took to the streets in celebration

News of the victory caused a sensation, but it was a mix of sadness and joy. Many read the casualty lists with keen attention, while others took to the streets in celebration ...

(although some radicals despaired at the triumph of the Tory general over the liberal hero, Napoleon). The battle soon became seen as a very British affair, with the Prussians' involvement relegated to a minor role – despite their numerical and strategic importance. As the century progressed, Waterloo became part of what Britain meant. Wellington did much to draw upon these connections, turning his London residence, Apsley House, into what almost amounts to a shrine to victory over Napoleon. The house, which had been designed by Richard Adam, was known as No. 1, London, on account of its location on Hyde Park Corner. In 1830, Wellington adapted the building to hold a ninety-foot 'Waterloo Gallery' that contained over a hundred paintings (many obtained from the King of Spain's collection). Here he hosted regular lavish Waterloo Dinners on the anniversary of the battle. In later years, the floor of the staircase was reinforced to contain a massive white-marble statue of Napoleon by Canova. Accounts of the battle, dioramas and prints continued to celebrate the battle. And indeed, it marked an important point, an end to the Napoleonic and revolutionary period of European history – at least for several generations. The support given to the role of the monarchy, especially constitutional monarchies, and to the idea of the balance of power and the role of international diplomacy helped to prevent a general war in Europe for a century.

At first, Waterloo posed problems of commemoration and to the imagination. The battlefield, like much of the surrounding countryside, was plain. The ruins of Hougoumont and La Haie Sainte remained, and were often the centre of depictions of the battle. An observation tower from the battle served as a viewing platform. Ghoulish souvenirs could be found for several years; three Essex lads found what they decided was a Frenchman's finger, which they pickled in spirits to take back as a memento. Tellingly, early prints and accounts of the

battle focused not only on the battle itself, but also on its bloody aftermath, showing corpses on the field or being interred in mass graves. Anecdotes of stoical wit, such as the loss of Lord Uxbridge's leg (he observed, following its amputation, that the surgeon's knife was rather blunt and informed the Marquise d'Assche, 'You see I shan't be able to dance with you any more except with a wooden leg'), took the place of attention to the interior suffering.

Sir Walter Scott – 'a very agreeable man, so full of anecdote', in Wellington's opinion – set the seal on his poetical career with a long poem on the victory at Waterloo, following a pilgrimage to the battlefield. He found the area lacking the grandeur needed for an epic poem. Wellington himself returned to the field on a number of occasions, but found the experience saddening and disquieting.

Much of the Duke's time at his headquarters at Cambrai was spent among glittering society, enjoying dinners, balls and theatricals. He was awarded the highest honours available from the courts of Europe, and could address princes as 'cousin'. Some of his favourite friends joined him, including Josephina Grassini, Lady Charlotte Greville, Lady Frances Wedderburn-Webster, and Lady Shelley, with whom he enjoyed riding and also gave a private tour of Malmaison, Josephine's mansion until her death. As she recalled, 'we had great fun in going through it, with two or three wretched candles.' The Duke's fondness for female company – he enjoyed letting his hair down with such high spirited women as Lady Caroline Lamb (he despised her attachment to Lord Byron) – gave much material to gossips. Rumours that the Duke's friendship with Lady Frances Wedderburn-Webster had gone beyond the bounds of propriety and that her husband was seeking redress from Wellington appeared in the British press in 1815. On reading the reports, the Duke, declared, 'That's too bad! The writer's a walking lie. Never saw her alone in my life. This must be checked.' Wellington's wish was answered, and a court found the newspaper's allegations false. He did, it seems fall for Marianne Patterson, the young wife of an American merchant, whom he took on a tour of the battlefield. It appeared to his close associates that he fell very much in love with her, and looked 'horribly ill' when she left for America. Following a divorce – and to the Duke's fury – she married Lord Wellesley (Richard) in 1816.

In October 1815 he returned to England to take a course of the sulphurated waters at Cheltenham for his rheumatism. The visit also included a round of victory dinners given by leading figures of the day, including the Prince Regent. He also took the opportunity to interfere in the affairs of the many young women in his circle: he attempted to reconcile William Lamb with Lady Caroline, and helped to re-establish her reputation in society. He offered marital advice to his niece and attempted unsuccessfully to obtain a bishopric for his brother Gerald. The leisurely pace of the spa relaxed him, and Kitty found him at his most pleasant. He also took time to play with the boys, Arthur and Charles. Despite his generally benign rule, the Duke had become a lightning rod for French dissatisfaction with foreign occupation and he was dubbed the 'tyrant of Cambrai'. On his return one night from a party, he was fired upon. The would-be assassin, a Napoleonist named Cantillon, was soon captured, but was acquitted by a French jury. Napoleon left the man 100,000 francs in his will. Another attempt on Wellington's life was thought likely, but he refused to alter his routine or to leave Paris, since that would 'give the most fatal shake to everything.'

Although he visited London several times, he remained in Paris until, in December 1818, he received the offer of the post of Master-General of the Ordnance, bringing with it the promise of a seat in the Cabinet. He accepted, and in the summer of 1819 returned to England to take up the post.

4

In 1815, Britain had won the war, but victory did not bring immediate prosperity. Wellington returned to a very different country from the one that he had left as a young officer in the 1790s.

In the service of the state

Wellington returned to Britain a hero, determined to serve his country in a political capacity. Having witnessed the effects of political infighting during his time in the Peninsula, and the effects it had on his brother Richard, the Duke was determined to rise above 'factiousness'; yet within a decade he was fighting in the political trenches. The political tumult led him to become one of the most hated men in Britain: stones were thrown at his house and he faced mobs in the street and was almost pulled from his horse. Perhaps perversely, Wellington, the Tory defender of hierarchy and privilege (albeit tempered by duty), unwittingly helped to usher in an era of unprecedented social and political reform. In the face of bitter, even violent, opposition from ultra-Tories, he removed the bar on Catholics holding political office – a prohibition that had existed since 1689. Following the collapse of the Tory party under his premiership (1828–1830), the Great Reform Act of 1832, which reorganized the electoral system, was introduced, to the surprise of all those involved.

In 1815, Britain had won the war, but victory did not bring immediate prosperity. Wellington returned to a very different country from the one that he had left as a young officer in the 1790s. Britain had been at war for a generation; indeed, the nation had begun to be defined by its military successes, but peace raised uncomfortable questions; unemployment rose dramatically as soldiers were discharged and military contracts came to an end. The political and social landscape had similarly been transformed; peace also brought questions about the state of the nation to the fore of public and private debate. Britain was no longer just a land of farmers and artisans living in small villages and towns. Rapidly expanding cities, notably Birmingham and Manchester, were creating a new urban mass and transforming established methods of small-scale industry. Machine-breaking and other acts of violence unsettled local magistrates, Irish

Previous page: Nineteenth-century
Wellington boots. Always interested
in his dress and averse to damp, in
1815 the Duke ordered two pairs of
boots higher than the half-length
boots he had made for the Peninsular
campaign. Made by Mr Hoby of
St James's, London, the style became
known as 'Wellington Boots'.
Museum of London

immigration and Nonconformist self-confidence challenged Anglican authority and radical dissent found new outlets in prints, pamphlets and mass protest, matched by new literacy.

Out of these changes three issues came to dominate the new political world and became Wellington's battles for the next decade and more. In 1815, tariffs protecting the price of corn and other foodstuffs had been introduced, ensuring a decent return for landowners, but, opponents argued, also keeping the price of bread artificially high. These Corn Laws contradicted the arguments for free trade proposed by exponents of the new economic thought, often influenced by the writings of Adam Smith. Corn became an issue around which radical and popular politics could assemble. In Ireland, as Wellington had noted as Chief Secretary before he left for the Peninsula, discontent at repression of Catholics and poverty was increasing, while in Britain calls for Catholic emancipation were growing. While he remained active, George III had forbidden any discussion of the Catholic question by his cabinet, and it had become the most painful of all the political sores, and one that refused to be bled or lanced. Finally, a more general political demand for 'reform' had begun to be voiced more forcibly. Parliament, many argued, no longer represented the people, particularly the newly powerful industrialists, merchants and urban workers.

As Master-General of the Ordnance, the Duke was in charge of the Royal Artillery, the officers of the Royal Engineers and certain ranks of the Royal Corps of Sappers and Miners (then still independent of the army, controlled from Horse Guards). Much of the work was taken care of by a secretary, leaving the Duke free to offer advice in cabinet, particularly on military matters and questions of civil order. (From 1819, Lord FitzRoy Somerset, the future Lord Raglan, Wellington's aide-de-camp and military secretary since the Peninsula, filled this position.) An appointment at this level cannily brought to Lord Liverpool's administration the cachet of Wellington's international reputation without upsetting other members of the cabinet by giving a Wellesley too prominent a post. The Duke cautiously accepted the position, making it clear that he considered himself free to rise above faction and to remain 'at liberty to take any line' he felt necessary. His experiences in the Peninsula had convinced him of the evils of unnecessary political dissent and parliamentary fighting.

Wellington also had a new home. Parliament had voted him £600,000 (which is approximately equivalent to £27 million today) for a residence suitable for the hero of the Peninsula, in a similar fashion to the Duke of Marlborough's Blenheim Palace a century before. After much searching in the shires during furloughs from his Continental duties, the Duke eventually settled on Stratfield Saye and its 5,000 Hampshire acres in 1817. It cost £263,000. Wellington planned to demolish the restrained white-stucco house and erect a 'Waterloo Palace' at the precisely calculated cost of £216,850 15s 3d. The building never materialized, and Stratfield Saye remained a pleasantly restrained country house, better suited as a base for hunting and riding than as an imposing memorial to martial triumph.

The Duke now had time to spend with his family, and Kitty noted a few happy trips around Hyde Park with her husband. But Wellington also missed the sociability of military life: he confided to Lady Shelley during a ball at Cambrai that he needed his house full, since 'for sixteen years I have always been at the head of our army, and I must have these gay fellows around me'. As compensation, London's social life welcomed him at the highest level. Regency England provided for a full week of balls, receptions and plays, and the 'Beau', as he had been nicknamed, added lustre to the social scene. Their marital quarrels came to a head around this time. Kitty was urged to wear some make-up, and she

Stratfield Saye on the Hampshire/
Berkshire border, home to the Dukes of
Wellington since 1817. A visitor found
the house 'not very comfortable, the
park ugly, the living mediocre, the
whole indeed indicating the lack of
sympathy existing between the Duke
and the Duchess.'
*Stratfield Saye. By permission of the
trustees of the Duke of Wellington*

complained about wearing a wig; it is clear that Wellington found other women
more attractive, as well as more intelligent and amusing. Kitty also bothered
Wellington with the details of housekeeping, about which she often managed to
get into minor muddles, finding it hard to meet all the expenses of the house.
Wellington was also probably difficult to live with; he could have little time for
the weakness and over-sensitivities of others and was used to living pretty much
as a bachelor while overseas. He wrote to his friend and confidante Harriet
Arbuthnot that he greatly regretted marrying Kitty.

The political classes were soon faced with a crisis. On 16 August 1819,

The Massacre, of Peterloo!, August 1819, by George Cruikshank. The killing of protesters gathered at St Peter's Field, Manchester, soon became known as 'Peterloo'. Wellington was popularly associated with the government's repressive responses to protest.
The British Museum, Sat. 13260

perhaps the largest crowd yet assembled for a political protest gathered in St Peter's Field in Manchester to hear Henry 'Orator' Hunt speak on Parliamentary reform. The meeting had raised great hopes among the radicals and other reformers, and for the first time ever, journalists had been dispatched from London to report on the event. The authorities were concerned, and Hunt's arrest was ordered. The riot act was read and then the local yeomanry, mounted on horseback and brandishing staves and the backs of their sabres, charged the crowd. Around four hundred were injured, not just by the militia but in the panic that ensued, and eleven people died. With an ironic nod to the Duke's victory in

Belgium, the bloody event was quickly dubbed the 'Peterloo Massacre' by radicals. It became a rallying point for reform. The establishment rallied behind the magistrates: the Regent congratulated the magistrates on their arrest of Hunt and the Government introduced six bills to outlaw similar dissent (known as the Six Acts). The Duke, who had little time for what he deemed to be the activities of an illegal mob, signed a letter of support for the magistrates, believing that they had acted appropriately at what was deemed an illegal assembly. He confided in a letter to Mrs Arbuthnot that the leaders should be hanged or revolution would be the result. As a prominent member of the government, Wellington was quickly associated in popular prints and papers with the massacre, and the popular memory of the Duke as the traitor of the Convention of Cintra quickly returned, thickened with a radical distaste for the loss of life of the Continental wars and liberal sympathy for Napoleon. Wellington found himself booed in the streets, and stones were thrown at Apsley House.

The Government's network of informers also uncovered, indeed encouraged, what became known as the 'Cato Street Conspiracy', organized by Arthur Thistlewood, a radical with a history of sedition. The conspirators planned to storm the cabinet's official dinner following the opening of parliament in February 1820 and shoot them all. Wellington proposed continuing as though the plot had not been uncovered, and suggested that the cabinet should wait for their attackers with hidden pistols and soldiers dressed as footmen. 'My colleagues, however,' the Duke later recalled to a friend, 'were of a different opinion, and perhaps they were right.' The dinner was moved and the would-be assassins were captured and convicted of treason. Thistlewood admitted he would rather have killed 'that damned villain' Wellington 'than any of them' and another conspirator disclosed that he planned 'to swear after the massacre that the Duke of Wellington turned out to be the biggest coward in the room, and begged for mercy on his knees.' James Ings, a bankrupt butcher, who brought two bags in which to take away the heads of Lord Castlereagh and Lord Sidmouth, also confessed to following Wellington, intending to plunge a knife into his back, but had been interrupted when the Duke met with FitzRoy Somerset and changed his route. The plotters attracted public support, and they were sentenced to death by hanging rather than being drawn and quartered. As it was, the hangman was publicly attacked and nearly castrated.

But by 1820, the political atmosphere had changed. The old King, George III, had died at last, and the Regent could finally be crowned. Shocked by the repressive measures taken at St Peter's Field and by the subsequent Six Acts, a middle class made afraid of reform by the Revolution in France became more amenable to gradual change; and the governing classes began to recognize that some modification of the order of things was required. The pro-reform *Manchester Guardian* (the *Guardian* of modern-day news-stands) was founded shortly after, and institutions such as London University began to provide an education to Nonconformists as well as to Anglicans. These changes, together with restrained use of troops and police measures, ensured that fears or hopes of revolution remained unrealized. The period demonstrated the government's ability to keep control, for which Wellington may take some credit for his suggestion that troops should not be dispersed across the country to repress every mob, but allowed some riots and looting to blow over.

The change in the country's mood can perhaps best be seen in the extraordinary divorce trial of Queen Caroline, which took place in Parliament in the autumn of 1820. The new King's attempt to prove adultery by his wife, who had been living a life of some extravagance on the Continent since 1814, became a focus for dissent. Historians debate whether the trial distracted the people from their grievances or provided a rallying point, but undoubtedly the trial ensured that the proper place for debate remained in Parliament and the press, rather than in riot and assassination. Wellington played an important role in the case. When King George IV acceded to the throne, he did not at all welcome the return of his estranged wife – indeed, he attempted to have her passport removed. The Whigs and radicals, on the other hand, rallied behind her, and stage-managed a dramatic return in June 1820. Wellington was sent to negotiate a deal in which she would receive £50,000 a year on condition that she live abroad and have her name removed from the Church of England's liturgy. She refused, and Wellington attracted more stones from the mob. The King decided to make use of the 'green bag', which contained the reports of witnesses to her indiscretions, and attempted to introduce a parliamentary bill 'of Pains and Penalties' in order to divorce her. According to the radical essayist William Hazlitt, the 'affair struck its roots into the heart of the kingdom'. Although the London crowd mostly took to mocking or praising the colourful cast of witnesses, particularly Teodoro Majocchi, the Queen's servant who testified against her, and whose response of 'Non mi ricordo' ('I don't remember') became the catchphrase of the day, they could also turn violent. At the end of August, Wellington was almost pulled from his horse and only just escaped. As a peer, Wellington – who was suffering from a cough and fever – was required to attend the debate in Parliament. By November the motion was defeated, and the Whigs and Radicals began to threaten revelations about George's own affairs. Furious at the outcome, the King determined to change his administration, but Wellington wrote to him to argue against it. George was irritated by a letter that Wellington 'ought not to have written to an equal, much less to his Sovereign', but took his advice.

In May 1821, Napoleon died on St Helena of what the doctors believed was a perforated, cancerous stomach. Wellington again had occasion to visit the site of Napoleon's defeat. In 1821, the King required the Duke to accompany him on a tour of the battlefield at Waterloo. It took place in the rain, and the King, the Duke said, 'took it all very coolly', and 'indeed never asked a single question, nor said one word, till I showed him where Lord Anglesey's leg was buried, and then he burst into tears.' (Sir Henry Paget, Earl of Uxbridge, was created Marquis of Anglesey in 1815.) A more personal loss struck Wellington the next year. By 1822, Wellington – and others – had become increasingly concerned by the paranoid and delusional state of Lord Londonderry (formerly Lord Castlereagh), one of Wellington's oldest friends and the current Foreign Secretary. After witnessing Londonderry's condition, the Duke offered to cancel a forthcoming trip to Flanders. Londonderry, who was being blackmailed by a male prostitute and his accomplices, refused; Wellington warned Londonderry's doctor 'that his mind is overpowered for the moment and labours under a delusion' before his departure. Lady Londonderry wrote to Wellington, informing him that 'I am sure you will be glad to hear that he saw Bankhead [his doctor] who ordered him to be cupped. The blood resembled jelly and he was instantly relieved. I have hopes that he will be well in a few days, but I really think he was upon the verge of a brain fever.' Bankhead wrote to Wellington, confirming this more hopeful prognosis. Despite these efforts, Londonderry became convinced that his wife and Wellington were plotting against him and became increasingly troubled. All pistols and knives were removed from the house, but after he summoned his doctor he opened an artery with a penknife that he kept in one of his dispatch boxes. He bled to death.

As well as the passing away of a friend, Wellington also suffered a physical loss. In August 1822, he was present in his capacity of the Master-General of

Ordnance at the testing of some new howitzers. The noise of the artillery led to pain and ringing in his left ear, for which a surgeon treated him with caustic soda, leading to further agonies: 'I never was so unwell, as I do not remember before in my life having passed a day in bed ... I was near fainting in the effort to dress myself, & was obliged to give it up. We are sad Creatures after all!' he wrote to Mrs Arbuthnot. He never recovered his hearing in the left ear and the damage to his inner ear led to a loss of balance which remained with him. His back teeth had also been lost during the Peninsular campaign, giving his cheeks a sunken appearance. At times, he could appear very unwell.

In the autumn of 1822, still suffering from poor health, Wellington was called upon to take Londonderry's place in the international congress that was being held at Verona and then Vienna. The congress aimed to confirm European peace, and the Tsar of Russia, the Emperor of Austria and the King of Prussia attended in person, together with scores of ambassadors and ministers. Once more among leading international society, Wellington advised on financial matters and spoke against foreign intervention in Spain, where the King had requested armed assistance against the liberals in order to avoid civil war. Wellington returned to London by Christmas, his health and balance once more troubling him. He suffered from sleeplessness and dizziness, fell down in the street and was almost run down; but, as a resolute bad patient and in opposition to his doctor's advice, he refused to cut back on his socializing and continued his round of dinners and visits to country houses. Wellington claimed to find the length of parties tedious, but clearly enjoyed being at the centre of things, close to political and personal gossip and unable to resist involving himself in the affairs of others; always, in Charles Greville's words, 'mixed up in messes.'

Foreign affairs continued to demand his time. In 1825, Canning, whom

Wellington claimed to find the length
of parties tedious, but clearly enjoyed
being at the centre of things, close to
political and personal gossip and
unable to resist involving himself in
the affairs of others ...

Wellington had suggested be appointed in Londonderry's place, proposed that
Wellington should visit Nicholas I, the new Tsar, in St Petersburg. Contemporaries
noted that he left his family and friends with unaccustomed emotion and even
tears. That they thought this so worthy of note is telling of his reputation for
emotional reticence. He arrived at the Russian capital in March 1826, writing
to Canning that he continued on his journey 'prosperously, and am quite well.'
George IV asked Canning to communicate to Wellington his happiness at
Wellington's success in 'ascertaining the politicks of the Court of St. Petersburg
at a moment so critical, and in laying the foundations of a good understanding
between His Majesty and the Emperor Nicholas, the effects of which may be
important in the highest degree, to the peace of the world.' The main questions of
the day were the Tsar's desire for a Continental congress (which Britain opposed)
and Russian support for Greek independence. Wellington managed to head off
calls for the congress, and agreed a measure of independence for Greece with
the support of Britain and Russia. Canning believed that Wellington had been
outwitted by the Russians, but the Duke believed he had played his best with a
weak hand; he was happy to return to London, and took pains not to forget gifts
for his female friends, such as a porphyry vase for Mrs Arbuthnot.

The months following his return were troubled. He was still suffering from
ill health, and Canning put it about that Wellington had failed in his mission in
Russia. His children were causing problems: Charles, 'full of tricks', had to be
removed from Trinity College, Cambridge for misbehaviour and Arthur, the
eldest, was listless and only managed to find interest in chatter and women.
Wellington set out a plan of conduct and reading, which included nearly a
hundred books, but suspected that it did little good. Relations with his brother
had not improved since his marriage to Marianne Patterson, with whom

Wellington had had a close friendship and possibly an affair. When the Duke of York died in January 1827, Wellington was appointed Commander-in-Chief, despite the King (who had began to imagine that he had himself been present at Salamanca) hankering after the post for himself. The health of the Prime Minister, Lord Liverpool, was also fading. Both Canning, who represented the moderate Tories, and Wellington, who could call on the support of right-wing Tories, were called to meet the King. The monarch appeared to be paying special attention to Wellington during the day, but as they were leaving, he kept Canning behind. Wellington later wrote to Canning asking who was to be Prime Minister, and received a withering reply. Furious at the rebuff, Wellington resigned his posts as Master-General of the Ordnance and Commander-in-Chief, and, if the contemporary cartoonists are right, sulked in Apsley House.

Canning, however, failed to recover from the rheumatic fever that he developed at the Duke of York's funeral and died that summer. Viscount Goderich formed a short-lived administration, but Wellington was soon seen, as his friend Gleig noted, as the 'acknowledged head of a great political party.' Wellington took care to spend the summer marshalling support during a series of house parties. He spoke before a series of crowds in large towns and took part in special balls and parades. By January 1828, Goderich's cabinet collapsed, and after sending Goderich away weeping, the King invited Wellington to form a government. The monarch had two caveats: Wellington was not to discuss Catholic emancipation, and Lord Grey, the Whig leader, could not be invited into the cabinet. On 22 January, Wellington held his first cabinet in Apsley House.

Wellington came to the post with a number of advantages, the greatest of which was his personal prestige. He descended from a respectable family, with a long lineage, but was not overwhelmingly aristocratic and had demonstrated enormous leadership and organizational brilliance during his military campaigns. Furthermore, he had extensive political experience, not only in Ireland, but in his capacity as ambassador and diplomat. His common sense and pragmatism allowed him to tackle problems effectively, and he could deal effectively with a demanding workload. Initially, he could count on support from the ultra-Tories, since he had not been tarred by serving under Canning and appeared to oppose Catholic emancipation. On the other hand, a series of personal and political faults worked against him. On a practical level, his deafness exacerbated his cool manner in conversation, and the loss of his back teeth affected his oratorical abilities. He respected the role of the monarchy, but did not get on well with the King in person. He gave orders well, but failed to operate a cabinet effectively and did not have experience of running the Commons. Most seriously, he lacked the personal drive to be Prime Minister – seeing it as a matter of duty more than ambition – and failed to understand or even appreciate the new demands posed by the changing nature of politics. Government was no longer about the elite, but had to accommodate the demands of public opinion.

The initial difficulty facing Wellington was that of his choice of cabinet colleagues. Robert Peel became Home Secretary, and advised Wellington to select a more liberal cabinet. As a conciliatory measure, Wellington selected four Canningites: William Huskisson as Secretary for War and the Colonies, Palmerston as Secretary at War (in charge of the administration of the army), Charles Grant as President of the Board of Trade and the eccentric Viscount Dudley and Ward as Foreign Secretary. The ultra-Tories remained outside. It was impolitic to include either of his own brothers, and he could only find a minor post for Mrs Arbuthnot's husband, Charles. After making these arrangements, he pointed out the piles of government boxes to Croker, exclaiming, 'There, there is

Opposite: *The Field of Battersea,*
21 March 1829, by William Heath.
One of many contemporary political
cartoons satirizing the Duke's
position on the Catholic question.
The Duke, wearing a monk's robe and
rosary, resembles a lobster claw –
slang for soldiers on account of their
red uniforms.
The British Museum, 15697

the business of the country, which I have not time to look at – all my time being employed in assuaging what gentlemen call their *feelings*. In short, the folly and unreasonableness of people are inconceivable.' The fragile nature of the Wellington–Canningite coalition soon became apparent, at first over the debate on a temporary relaxation of the Corn Laws, and then over the governance of two particularly rotten boroughs. Huskisson finally resigned over this issue.

The Catholic question quickly came to the fore. In May 1828, Sir Francis Burdett carried a motion in the Commons noting that the laws regarding Roman Catholics should be reconsidered. Then, in June, Daniel O'Connell, the Irish political activist and founder of the Catholic Association, stood as a candidate at the County Clare by-election. O'Connell won by a large majority, but as a Catholic he could not take his seat in Parliament. Throughout Ireland, discontent simmered. Catholics and Protestants began arming themselves, and Wellington, who had previously stated his opposition to reform, began to see that some measure of emancipation was required to avoid civil war; after weeks of tortured deliberation, he wrote to Mrs Arbuthnot: 'This state of things cannot be allowed to continue'. Some reform had already been put in place, this time satisfying the demands of the Nonconformists: in spring the Test and Corporation Acts, which limited membership of town corporations and civil and military offices to Anglicans, were repealed. Wellington spent the summer recuperating at Cheltenham spa and preparing the way for a Catholic Relief Bill, which he referred to as a 'rightabout face'. By January 1829, he had persuaded the King that the Cabinet could at least discuss the matter. The King's fierce-looking brother, the Duke of Cumberland, caught wind of the proposed reform and travelled from Germany to London to ensure that a firm Protestant line held. Wellington made it clear that the King would have to form a new government if Cumberland

remained in the country. Finally, Wellington had to threaten the King – who he believed had come close to madness by the way he rambled and fretted – with resignation before he granted approval to the bill.

Public opinion had also been whipped into a frenzy by the press; the ferocious cartoons and caricatures of the day demonstrate the depth of feeling the issue raised. Opposition in Parliament could also be fierce, the strongest of which came from the ultra-Tory wing of his own party. The whole matter exhausted Wellington. Oddly enough, some form of relief came in the actions of George Finch-Hatton, 9th Earl of Winchilsea and 4th Earl of Nottingham. Winchilsea charged Wellington with constructing 'an insidious design for the infringement of our liberties and the introduction of Popery into every department of State.' The Earl refused to apologize, and Wellington demanded a duel. Wellington again placed himself in the firing line.

On the morning of 21 March 1829, the Duke waited with his second, Sir Henry Hardinge, and a box of duelling pistols on Battersea Fields. He asked Hardinge to measure the ground and place Winchilsea, following the Duke's orders not to 'stick him up so near the ditch. If I hit him he will tumble in.' The two men found their positions, and the order to fire was given. Wellington, a notoriously bad shot, aimed wide. Winchilsea fired in the air before offering an

Previous pages: Walmer Castle, Kent, from *Apsley House and Walmer Castle*. As Lord Warden of the Cinque Ports (a sinecure with largely ceremonial duties) Wellington was allowed use of Walmer Castle as his official residence. The Duke found the Castle 'delightful', and much preferred it to Stratfield Saye. *The British Library, Maps 149.d.9*

apology to the Duke. The whole affair cheered Wellington up enormously, and temporarily swung the London mob, which was usually anti-Catholic, onto his side. On 13 April, the bill was passed.

This success elevated the Duke in the popular imagination once more. Cartoonists showed him as 'The Man wot drives the Sovereign'. The summer of 1829 also saw the introduction of Peel's Metropolitan Police, with strong support from Wellington. He was appointed Lord Warden of the Cinque Ports, a position that offered further prestige and use of Walmer Castle in Kent, of which he became greatly fond. But the Duke still suffered from ill health, particularly dizziness, causing him to fall from his horse, narrowly avoiding being crushed by a passing carriage. The efforts of guiding the Catholic bill through Parliament had physically exhausted him, while agricultural depression and continued Parliamentary warfare sapped his administration's strength: many believed that it would not hold together for long. Wellington himself confessed to Mrs Arbuthnot that he considered stepping aside for Peel to take his place.

On 26 June 1830, the King, suffering from obesity and numerous addictions, passed away. Wellington acted as an executor, and had to deal with several delicate questions, including burning the evidence of the King's secret marriage to Maria Fitzherbert. Another death took place in September, when the Duke travelled to Manchester to witness the opening of the Liverpool–Manchester railway. As the train stopped to take on water, he shook hands with Huskisson, the local MP and Wellington's political rival. Then, to everyone's horror, the heavy-set and slow-moving Huskisson was hit by Stephenson's Rocket, which was approaching from the other direction. The locomotive crushed his leg – witnesses heard the bones snap – and he died in agony shortly after, crying before he did so, 'It's all over with me; bring me my wife and let me die.' Wellington developed a life-long mistrust of the railways. Huskisson's loss also shook up Parliamentary alignments, since his death denied the Canning's old followers a leader to shepherd them, in Elizabeth Longford's words, 'back into the Tory fold'. Wellington was unable to accede to their demands for parliamentary reform.

Revolution was once more in the air. In France, the crowd again set up barricades in the Paris streets, and the French King Charles X renounced his crown in favour of Louis-Philippe in what became known as the 'July Days'. ('I was surprised', noted the Duke, 'about Charles the Tenth'; he believed him a 'man of action'. He found Louis-Philippe a 'monstrous able fellow, much abler than is commonly supposed, but a —') Revolution spread to Belgium, which demanded independence from the Netherlands. Disturbances also troubled the English countryside. Hayricks were set alight and new threshing machines were broken, and landowners began to petition for a stern response. The Duke had little time for those who were frightened by what he saw as the manifestations of a few troublemakers. But the recent elections had unsettled the government, and Whig politicians such as Henry Brougham (pronounced 'broom') had helped to whip up demands for reform. The political realignment that resulted from the inclusion of Catholics in the electorate led, in some contemporaries' and historians' opinion, to demands for some sort of constitutional readjustment as a Protestant counterweight. The irony was not lost on Wellington. Demands for representation for the cities, the abolition of pocket boroughs (constituencies with very few voters and controlled by a patron) and an end to the political dominance of the great landowners had become a rallying point for thousands. The more liberal Tories found themselves given succour by public opinion.

Palmerston and other Canningite politicians made the best of their new-found strength and battled the Duke for influence within the new cabinet that followed the general election after George IV's death. The Duke remained firm in his opposition to reform, which he believed would lead to the unnecessary unravelling of British society: 'I shall therefore at all times and under all circumstances oppose it.' The question came to a great debate in Parliament in November. In response to an allusion by Lord Grey to reform, the Duke stoutly defended the constitution as it existed. He refused to answer calls for reform; the house responded in uproar. 'I have not said too much, have I?' the Duke asked Aberdeen when he sat down. 'You'll hear of it,' answered Aberdeen. Despite this question, the Duke had drawn a line in the sand, and had done so intentionally. He had to bring the matter to a head. He firmly believed in the providence of the British constitution; his experience on the Continent and contemporary events confirmed in his mind that reform only brought violence and dissatisfaction. Despite all its flaws, Parliament, he believed, was able to adapt to contemporary demands, and was able to represent all sections of society. While some boroughs were indeed 'rotten', as a whole the system worked well, and could represent the interests of landowners, newly rich merchants and nabobs of the East India Company alike. The only alternative he perceived was anarchy and the rule of the mob.

The effect of the speech in the country was electric. Letters poured in, offering support or vitriol. The London streets were filled with angry crowds, and the Duke became once again the focus for popular hatred. Apsley House had to be shuttered with iron bars (providing one possible source for the nickname 'Iron Duke') and provided with armed guards in every room. Finally, Wellington postponed the Lord Mayor's banquet, fearing that the necessary display of troops would lead to violence. Ironically, the military leader's decision not to deploy force demonstrated to all but the most loyal that his administration was being swept away by events. On 15 November, the government was defeated by twenty-nine votes on a hostile motion to scrutinize the Civil List. Brougham's parliamentary reform motion was due to be debated the next day, and to avoid greater indignity, Wellington resigned as Prime Minister.

The Duke had faced enormous challenges during his premiership. A series of crises that had been delayed by government inaction or postponement demanded the attention of the brisk, matter-of-fact commander. He had often coped well with them, but the overthrow of his government a mere three months after triumphing in a general election cast him in a poor light. The popular antipathy to his premiership soon returned as he fought reform from the opposition benches and the image of the unbending iron Tory patriarch came to dominate assessments of his leadership. Despite his energy and industriousness, as his premiership continued Wellington became, in the words of a recent historian, an 'increasingly sceptical recipient or listener; and less and less given to encouraging responses.' His reputation for a stoical attitude towards patronage stemmed in part from the fact that he had less to give than did previous leaders of the government; the pot of civil patronage had been skimmed by his predecessors or debased by the profligate distribution of peerages or other honours. He attended assiduously to the business of the House of Lords, rarely missing a debate, although his contribution suffered from lack of oratorical polish and poor diction. Others found his debating style much like the man: firm and to the point. He acted wisely and bravely on the Catholic question, but was unable to square reform with his principles, which included a sophisticated view of the responsiveness and rights of Parliament and of the prerogatives of the King; it seems unlikely that another course could have kept the Tories intact for as long as he did. Nonetheless, he failed to recognize that it was no longer the King who made Prime Ministers, but party and public opinion.

5

5

In the absence of a modern party
system, Wellington shared the view
that strong government would be
impossible without the guiding
hand of a few aristocratic families.

Elder statesman

In January 1832, the Earl of Stanhope visited Stratfield Saye, where the Duke
showed him 'his new apparatus for warming the house by tubes of hot water.'
The Duke could tell him the exact cost of his new central heating: including
fitting it amounted to £219. In contrast to his support for many such ingenious
inventions (steam locomotives and new-fangled artillery pieces excepted), the
Duke stood firmly opposed to political innovation. Following the collapse of his
administration, the Duke mounted a last defence against reform from the House
of Lords, where he was able to command a majority. Parliament, in his view,
should represent all classes of men, particularly 'the first men of all professions,
in all branches of trade and manufacture, connected with our colonies and
settlements abroad': it was a mistake to place Parliament 'under popular influence'
as proposed, he believed, by Lord Grey and Lord John Russell. The House of
Commons passed Russell's Reform Bill three times, which the Lords then
rejected. Wellington warned that the introduction of the bill would 'date the
downfall of the Constitution'. In the absence of a modern party system,
Wellington shared the view that strong government would be impossible without
the guiding hand of a few aristocratic families. Furthermore, pocket boroughs
would be abolished without compensation for the owners of what was seen as
a form of personal – and very expensive – property.

    A rapid series of political events and popular agitation known as the 'May
Days' caused many to fear revolution: there was a run on the Bank of England
and a second Peterloo or worse was feared. Riots had broken out across the
country in response to the Lords' overturning of the reform bills: in some of the
worst, in Bristol, several hundred were killed during the fires and looting caused
by the mob. As a staunch opponent of reform, Wellington was as unpopular as he
had ever been. Popular cartoons and pamphlets lampooned him as the arch-Tory,

determined to spike the wheels of progress. His postbag brought death-threats.
Mobs once again threw stones and rubbish at the window of Apsley House: at
one point a stone smashed through the window behind the Duke as he worked
at a desk. On 17 May, William IV declined to create fifty new peers in order to
break the deadlock in the Lords, and Grey's administration resigned. Wellington
was asked to form a new administration, but was unable to muster enough
support, and so, in the interests of stable government, on 7 June 1832 the Reform
Bill was allowed to pass. Bills for Scotland and Ireland soon followed. The Duke's
role in stalling the bill was not forgotten by the crowd. On 18 June, he was
caught by a mob on his way home from a sitting with the medallist Beneditto
Pistrucci at the Mint, but aided by two Chelsea Pensioners and some policemen
and defended by a buggy to the rear, he coolly rode home.

Viewed from a modern perspective, the Reform Act left much of the
political system unaltered: the franchise remained strictly limited; new cities such
as Birmingham, Leeds, and Manchester still had far fewer representatives than
their populations warranted; some fifty pocket boroughs remained; the electorate
doubled from 409,000 to 814,000, but over three-quarters of the adult male
population remained disenfranchised. The vote was not extended to women
(and indeed, voters were defined as 'male persons' for the first time). Yet reform
was seen as a historical landmark by the reformers and radicals. Historians
continue to argue about the extent of change ushered in by the bill and whether
it was necessary to avert revolution. Yet the bill certainly represented a significant
symbolic victory for reform, one that shaped the political landscape for years to
come. For his part, Wellington knew when to retreat. He continued to see the
reforms as ill-conceived, but he could not allow the fatal undermining of the
crown in the popular mind risked by political deadlock. On the opening session

of the new Parliament, he made a snobbish, but politically acute, observation on the new class of politician, remarking on the prevalence of 'shockingly bad hats'.

As Wellington fought these political battles, Kitty descended further into ill-health. She had often suffered from a weak constitution, but by early 1832, it was clear that she was dying. Her final disease has not been diagnosed, but was probably either a form of cancer or cholera. She lay in her room at Apsley House, proudly surrounded by the trophies of her husband's triumphs. Wellington stayed by her bedside to the last. She died on 24 April. It was strange, he noted afterwards, that people could live together for years, but could 'only understand one another at the end'.

In contrast, he found intimacy and understanding in the company of Harriet Arbuthnot. Contrary to persistent rumours, it seems that their affection for each other did not develop into a sexual relationship, but he found her a continual source of support, friendship and political conversation, and the news of her death in autumn 1833 struck him a hard blow. The letter informing him of the loss fell from his hands and he collapsed, distraught, onto a nearby sofa, but, mindful as ever of his duty, he mounted his horse and rode to commiserate her widower. Charles returned to live with Wellington.

The Duke had also found himself entangled in another complicated female relationship. In late 1833 Anna Maria Jenkins, a pious, attractive young woman, wrote to the Duke, meaning to give him a 'new birth into righteousness' and entered into a long-running correspondence. Only since the twentieth century have historians accepted the authenticity of their surviving letters, which were found in the attic of a 'country house within thirty miles of New York'. These letters reveal an odd mixture of initial attraction, religiosity, obsession and irritation. On their first meeting in 1834, she admired the Duke's 'beautiful silver head', and for his part, the Duke declared: 'Oh, *how* I *love* you! *How* I *love* you.' He enquired whether she would be prepared to become a duchess. Something – whether an unwelcome sexual advance from either party or a clumsy attempt at his religious conversion by her is uncertain – damaged their early friendship, but the connection survived and they continued to correspond by letter for the remainder of his life.

Wellington also had a public role outside of the Lords, as well as a busy social calendar. He had been appointed Constable of the Tower of London in 1826: he ordered the removal of foul-smelling sewage from the moat, demanded that the Tower's doctor either work or resign his post and decided to appoint the Yeoman warders – commonly known as 'Beefeaters' – from amongst the ranks of former non-commissioned officers. As Lord Lieutenant of Hampshire since 1820, responsible for military defence and the maintenance of order in the county, the Duke found himself confronted by the hayrick-burning activities of 'Captain Swing', the fictitious leader of rioting agricultural labourers. The 'Captain' had started his work in Hampshire by setting the Duke's pew in Stratfield Saye church alight. Wellington, he recorded, 'induced the magistrates to put themselves on horseback, each at the head of his own servants and retainers, grooms, huntsmen, game-keepers armed with horse-whips, pistols, fowling pieces and what they could get, and to attack in concert if necessary, or singly, these mobs, disperse them, destroy them, and take and put in confinement those who could not escape. This was done in a spirited manner'. In 1834, he accepted the Chancellorship of Oxford University, and took his duties very seriously, although he strove to avoid speaking Latin wherever possible – in contrast to his brother's facility with the classics – and worried that he made a fool of himself during University ceremonies because of his uncertain pronunciation of that language.

Wellington also had a public role
outside of the Lords, as well as a
busy social calendar.

At the end of his life he was called upon to make an important contribution to
the Royal Commission on Universities. Warning against overly radical reforms,
he supported the changes proposed in the final report.

In November 1834, at the age of sixty-five, as he was prepared to ride out
for some sport, the Duke received a summons from the King who asked him
to form an administration. He agreed with some reluctance, but only on the
condition that he would serve until Peel, who was away in Italy, returned and
took over the role. Wellington's second premiership, or 'dictatorship' as he referred
to it, lasted only a matter of weeks, and on Peel's arrival he stepped down to
become Foreign Secretary. His tenancy in this office was again brief and not
particularly happy. He found himself obliged to follow the policies and alliances
of his predecessor, Lord Palmerston, and his appointment of the Marquess of
Londonderry – a resolute Tory and outspoken critic of reform – as the
Ambassador at St Petersburg caused outrage in the Commons and undermined
the government. By 8 April 1835, Peel's administration was out of office.

In 1837, King William IV died, and Victoria ascended to the throne. At first,
she surrounded herself with Whigs; on one occasion Wellington, in his capacity as
Chancellor of Oxford, was the only Tory present at a court banquet. In 1839, the
Queen was horrified at the resignation of Melbourne's Whig government. On
Melbourne's advice, she summoned Wellington, who had known her since birth,
but, at the age of seventy, he declined to accept the office of Prime Minister for
the third time. When the Duke voted against increasing the allowance to her
future husband, Prince Albert of Saxe-Coburg and Gotha, she determined never
to speak to him again or invite him to her wedding. Melbourne, however,
persuaded her to, since the nation expected the Duke to be present at such an
event. Relations thawed. Wellington changed his mind about the matter of the

allowance, and supported the Queen when she decided in the face of opposition from the royal family to appoint Prince Albert as sole regent in the event of her death. He also assisted in encouraging the emigration of Sir John Conroy, whom she hated as a result, Wellington believed, of being her mother's lover. (Such encouragement involved 'plenty of butter', Wellington told his friend Greville.) By the summer of 1840, Wellington had become a favourite with her. She visited him at Walmer Castle and at Stratfield Saye, and she began to rely on him for advice on constitutional matters. For his part, he felt as duty-bound as ever to support the position of the monarch.

Wellington faced a final battle on the home front. In 1848, news of revolutions on the Continent compounded the establishment's fears of domestic agitation. The Chartists, a mass political movement that campaigned for an extension of the franchise to the middle classes and working men, had arranged a mass rally in London; the dining rooms of the rich were full of rumours of revolutions and the mob. Wellington reassured the Queen that all necessary measures had been put in place; volunteer militia were formed and the army made extensive preparations. In the event, the rally passed off peacefully.

Despite his noticeably failing health, Wellington continued to devote himself to another of his appointments, that of Commander-in-Chief. Of all his public positions, this undoubtedly gave him the most satisfaction, yet he had been strongly criticized for failing to introduce necessary military reforms. As at the outbreak of the Revolutionary Wars in 1792, in the Crimea in 1854, the British army found itself facing its enemy with the equipment, training and structures of the army of the previous generation. Thousands of British soldiers died, needlessly, as a consequence of poor sanitary conditions and confused logistics. The frail and aged Duke had neither the strength nor the inclination to put in

place the necessary reforms that he might have encouraged as a young man; he
was also criticized for igniting the 'Invasion Scare' of 1847, when he suggested
that the south coast was ill-prepared to resist a French attack. The result was
increased tension between the two nations and the construction of expensive,
and unnecessary, defences in the 1850s.

As Ranger of the Royal Parks, the Duke took a keen interest in the Great
Exhibition of 1851, which he worried risked rallying mobs and ruining Hyde
Park. He made detailed plans for the protection of Buckingham Palace,
Parliament and the new exhibition, and remained suspicious of the glass
construction of the 'Crystal Palace'. The story that he answered the Queen's

worries about sparrows inside the Crystal Palace with the droll words, 'Try
sparrowhawks, Ma'am,' is, unfortunately, apocryphal. (The pithy Wellingtonian
phrase 'publish and be damned' – his response to Harriette Wilson's attempt to
blackmail him in 1824 – is also of similarly dubious provenance.) On 1 May 1851,
the Duke, riding in a very stiff-backed manner, officially entered the 'Palace' and
made a tour of the myriad exhibitions. By now the Duke's public image had
changed somewhat from that of the hate-figure of the mob and the penny-press. It
was his birthday, and the crowd cheered him round the glass halls. He became a

convert to the exhibition, and was
regularly seen there strolling. Another
delight remained his grandchildren, niece
and nephews, and their young friends.
While he could, he indulged in pillow-
fights and other games at Walmer Castle,
and enjoyed the company of the young.

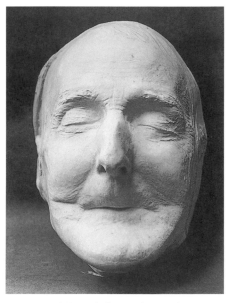

By the end of his life, his age and
his attempts to rise above the
factiousness of politics, together with
the continued public memory of his
military victories gave Wellington the
presence of an elder statesman. The
'Iron Duke' had become a respected,
and even loved, pillar of state.

On the morning of 14 September 1852, a maid found the Duke 'making
a great noise'. An apothecary was summoned and when he arrived Wellington
complained of 'some derangement' in his chest. The apothecary felt his pulse and
suggested an ammonia stimulant and a little tea and toast. When his valet offered
some tea, the Duke replied, 'Yes, if you please.' These were his final words: after
drinking the tea, the Duke fell into a fit and passed out; a mustard emetic was
applied, poultices placed on his arms and legs and a feather was brushed against
his jaw: to no avail. Wellington was carefully placed on his favourite chair, but
he fell deeper into unconsciousness. At around three thirty in the afternoon, the
doctor's son placed a mirror in front of the Duke's mouth: it remained unfogged.
The Duke was dead.

Wellington's funeral car. Over eighteen
tons in weight and twenty feet long,
the carriage had to be drawn by twelve
dray horses. At one point, its wheels
sank into a hole, requiring the efforts
of sixty policemen to pull it clear.
The British Library, HS 74/1739

Although his age and state of health meant his death could not have caused much surprise, his loss was widely and deeply felt. As Queen Victoria recorded in her diary, 'one cannot think of this country *without "the Duke"*'. The Queen and Prince Consort determined that his funeral would be delayed until after the return of Parliament in November, partly to allow time for the extensive preparations to be made. His body was embalmed, a death mask prepared and locks of his hair were taken and passed to friends and family as a solemn memento, and even his false teeth were presented as a souvenir.

As part of the funeral procession, the Duke's groom led his master's old horse with Wellington's boots reversed. This 'touching sight' moved the Queen to tears.
The British Library, HS 74/1739

Wellington's funeral remains one of the greatest of state occasions. At first, his coffin lay at Walmer Castle. Some 7,000 people filed past. Then, after the sounding of guns, the body was taken to London and escorted by Life Guards to the black-cloth-draped Great Hall of Chelsea Hospital, the site of the inquiry after the Convention of Cintra. Here he lay in state, surrounded by spears wrapped in black velvet and laurel wreaths under a silver-lined black canopy. The crowds were immense, and seven people were reported killed in the crush. A million people thronged the London streets on 18 November as the lengthy funeral procession slowly paraded to St Paul's. A special funeral car had been fashioned, in part from cannon captured at Waterloo. The massive carriage was covered in national and martial decoration in a lavish style that was not to everyone's taste (Thomas Carlyle considered it the 'abominably ugliest' thing); it even included a mechanism to lower itself when it passed under the Temple Bar. It took twelve horses to pull the eighteen-ton cart, and sailors had to pull it up Ludgate Hill. The huge procession included 3,000 infantry, eight squadrons of cavalry, a private from each regiment and representatives from across Europe (and even Napoleon's illegitimate son, Count Alexandre Walewski, who was then the French envoy extraordinary to London). A particularly 'touching sight', one that brought tears to the Queen's eyes, was Wellington's groom leading the Duke's horse, a pair of Wellington boots hanging symbolically upside down. Eventually, the procession reached St Paul's. The 10,000 mourners in and around the cathedral then had to wait for an hour in the chill wind while the bearers struggled with the mechanism to transfer the coffin from the cart to a bier. (Some two hundred 'conveniences', supplied with looking glasses and combs, were available for the guests' comfort.) After a lengthy ceremony, the coffin was lowered into its tomb while the 'Dead March' was played (fittingly, other music used during the ceremony had been composed by Lord Mornington, the Duke's father). Then the Garter King of Arms read out the long list of his titles and Wellington's broken staff of office was thrown into the grave. Finally, the guns of the Tower fired a salute and trumpets sounded 'wail' from the West Door.

In 1857 a competition was held for a massive monument to Wellington within St Paul's Cathedral. Alfred Stevens' giant memorial, with a recumbent effigy of the dead Duke, won the prize and was completed in 1878 – a bronze equestrian statue was finally added in 1912 (this was initially considered unsuitable

Plaster and wax model, by Alfred Stevens, of the Wellington Monument in St Paul's Cathedral. It is the largest monument in the cathedral.
Victoria and Albert Museum, 44-1878

for its ecclesiastical setting). The memorial was planned for the north aisle, but now still dominates the south-west chapel, the largest memorial in the cathedral. Elsewhere in London, the Wellington Arch stands outside Apsley House, at first topped by Matthew Cotes Wyatt's statue of Wellington astride a horse named Rosemary (not Copenhagen) until it was moved to Constitution Hill in 1882 and then to the military home of Aldershot. Richard Westmacott's bronze sculpture of Achilles commemorating his victories stands in Hyde Park, which caused enormous controversy when it was erected in 1822: it was the first time a nude had been used for an official statue and, furthermore, had been subscribed for by his 'countrywomen'; after a public outcry, a discreetly placed leaf was added to the design. Other statues had sprung up across Britain and were added to after his death.

Wellington's place in the Victorian imagination was assured. His public commemoration in brass and stone, together with the naming of streets, squares and even towns after his title and victories served as a physical reminder of Britain's brilliant military commander. For a time, Waterloo Day was marked by holidays, although this declined to a half-day in many schools and factories. Waterloo Dinners were arranged across the country, and in some parishes the bells continued to be rung on the anniversary of the battle of 18 June for many years; in some this remains the case. The Duke's slow retreat from active politics, his ties with Queen Victoria and association with national events such as the Great Exhibition dulled for many the memory of Wellington as the supporter of the Peterloo magistrates or the anti-Chartist. In contrast to Nelson, his public and private career found itself more suitable to nineteenth-century attitudes, and the publication of a mass of memoirs, anecdotes and conversations with the Duke served to place him firmly within the public mind. Unlike those of the victor of Trafalgar, his extramarital affairs largely stayed out of the public eye, and his determination, defence of common sense and pragmatism appealed to a certain sense of Englishness. Wellington also suited Britain's increasingly military and imperial self-image. Growing imperial and nationalistic rivalries with the Continental powers, particularly France, also suggested a comparison between Wellington and Napoleon. In school-books and speeches, the Duke became an object lesson on the British virtues of preparation, determination and common sense, while the 'little corporal' remained a warning against the perils of French egoism, abstract ideals and over-indulgent genius.

Military historians remain impressed by the Duke's martial abilities, particularly his ability to 'read the ground' tactically, control his troops and master logistical detail. Assaye and Salamanca demonstrated that Wellington could attack as well as defend brilliantly. After Salamanca, one of his French opponents, Maximilien Foy, believed his reputation had been raised 'almost to the level of Marlborough'. It is a fitting comparison: like Marlborough, Wellington fought expeditionary warfare and had to work within coalitions; both became entangled with Continental and domestic politics. In Europe, Wellington's reputation remains mixed: the Peninsular War caused enormous suffering and encouraged

Front of Apsley House, London, at dusk. No. 1, London, remains the London home of the Dukes of Wellington but ten rooms are open to the public as the Wellington Museum.
Victoria and Albert Museum, 36161

lasting instability in Portugal and Spain; Waterloo is seen as something of a near-defeat only rescued by Blücher and his German troops and remains linked to Napoleon far more than to Wellington.

Wellington's reputation as a politician did not initially weather well. While admiring his anti-factional ideals, historians were quick to see him as a soldier out of his depth, unable to adapt to the undoubted changes in British society and politics, although he remained a source of good counsel to the Queen and others. More recently, his political abilities have been reassessed by historians. While he ultimately lacked the empathy and insight into the needs of the new, industrialized Britain, he performed reasonably well in cabinet, tackling problems with determination and common sense. Despite his reputation as an autocrat, he was able to compromise, and he ushered in the Catholic Relief Act and helped to abolish the Corn Laws, anathemas to fellow Tories, and of great consequence for the course of British history. Confronted by the irreconcilable demands of the ultra-Tories and those with more Whiggish views, he found a path through the political mire, at the risk of his own career.

Such sacrifices lay at the heart of the Duke's public image. He stood, as

Samuel Smiles argued in *Self-Help* (1859), for self-denial, patriotism and persistence. He retained a quiet, but deeply held, sense of Anglican religious conviction and duty. He avoided the trappings of fuss and cant and advocated simplicity, fairness and frankness. He greatly preferred the hunting field to the drawing room. The many women in his life found he had little small-talk. Many other contemporaries found him gruff, even to the point of rudeness, and found that he could have a temper. Although Wellington was in many ways a representative of the old order of things, the public presentation of his private characteristics made him – no doubt against his will – very much a modern man. The steam-press, consumer culture (his recognizable 'Nosey' silhouette appeared on innumerable plates, shaving brushes and other mass-produced artefacts) and the beginnings of popular politics made the Duke into what we might today consider labelling as a brand.

Yet despite posterity's preservation of Wellington's character as the 'Iron Duke' (a nickname probably first given in *Punch* magazine in 1845), the real man was undoubtedly a far more complex creature, the centre of whom undoubtedly sought affection. He sailed to India with a trunk filled with romantic literature as well as military history; he enjoyed the company of women, but found himself in a deeply unhappy marriage. As such a public figure, Wellington was profoundly aware of his image. Disinclined towards the need for popular approval – he believed in aristocratic government rather than democracy – he nonetheless recognized the need to generate a public persona and was aware of the power of anecdote or the well-turned remark for sticking in the public imagination. He dressed stylishly, and enjoyed cutting a figure, but disliked ostentation. His sons found him cool, but the Duke found he could play for hours with his grandchildren. There were many who were recipients of his kindness, or witnessed him in tears at the loss of a friend. He was also no doubt a difficult man to live with or work for. He was prone to sulks, could be petulant, failed to delegate and had a short temper. Despite these flaws – or perhaps to some extent because of them – Wellington altered the course of British history. British India's history cannot be written without noting the tipping of the scales of British involvement by the Wellesley brothers. In Europe, although Napoleon might well have been defeated without Arthur Wellesley's intervention, Britain's sense of national destiny and martial potency would have been very different. The Victorian Briton, certain of his imperial importance and defining characteristics, can hardly be imagined without him.

Chronology

1 April: Elected MP for Rye, Sussex
10 April: Marriage to Kitty Pakenham in Dublin
1807 3 February: Birth of first son (Arthur Richard)
3 April: Enters government as Chief Secretary of Ireland
31 July–30 September: Expedition to Copenhagen
1808 16 January: Birth of second son (Charles)
25 April: Appointed Lieutenant General
12 July: Appointed temporary command of expedition to Portugal
17 August: Battle of Roliça
21 August: Battle of Vimeiro
31 August: Convention of Cintra
November: Court of Inquiry
1809 Returns to take command in Portugal
12 May: Capture of Oporto
27–28 July: Battle of Talavera
4 September: Created Viscount Wellington of Talavera
1810 27 September: Battle of Bussaco
Autumn: Withdrawal behind Lines of Torres Vedras
1811 3–5 May: Battle of Fuentes de Oñoro
5–12 May: First siege of Badajoz
11 May: Surrender of Almeida
19 May–10 June: Second siege of Badajoz
Summer–Autumn: retreat to Portugal
1812 8–19 January: Siege of Ciudad Rodrigo
February: Becomes Earl of Wellington and Grandee of Spain
16 March–6 April: Third siege of Badajoz
22 July: Battle of Salamanca
18 August: Made Marquess of Wellington
19 September–21 October: Siege of Burgos
22 October: Retreats to Portugal
1813 21 June: Battle of Vitoria
25 July: Siege of San Sebastián
10 November: Battle of the Nivelle

	December: Battles of the Nive and St Pierre
1814	Enters France
	27 February: Battle of Orthez
	6 April: Napoleon abdicates
	10 April: Battle of Toulouse; end of the Peninsular War; travels to Paris
	3 May: Created Duke of Wellington
	24 May–8 June: Mission to Madrid
	5 July: Ambassador to the French Court
1815	3 February: Wellington British Plenipotentiary at Congress of Vienna
	7 March: News of Napoleon's escape from Elba reaches Vienna
	28 March: Wellington leaves Congress
	16 March: Battles of Ligny and Quatre Bras
	17 June: Wellington arranges forces on ridge of Mont-St-Jean
	18 June: Battle of Waterloo
	22 October: Commander-in-Chief of Army of Occupation in France
1818	10 February: attempt on his life by Cantillon
	26 December: Appointed Master-General of the Ordnance
1819	16 August: Peterloo Massacre in Manchester; repressive government measures
1820	23 February: Cato Street Conspiracy foiled
	Summer to Autumn: Trial of Queen Caroline
	19 December: Appointed Lord-Lieutenant of Hampshire
1821	5 May: Death of Napoleon on St Helena
1822	5 August: Damage to ear leads to partial deafness
	12 August: Suicide of Londonderry
	October–November: Representative at Congress of Verona
1826	February–April: Mission to the Court of St Petersburg, Russia
	29 December: Appointed Constable of the Tower of London
1827	5 January: Appointed Commander-in-Chief
1828	9 January: Prime Minister
	March–May: Repeal of Test and Corporation Acts
	20 May: Huskisson and Canningites resign from government
	1 August: Raises Catholic Question with King George IV

1829	20 January: Appointed Warden of the Cinque Ports
	21 March: Duel with Winchilsea on Battersea Common over the Catholic Question
	13 April: Catholic emancipation
1830	16 November: Resigns as Prime Minister; continues to oppose reform from the Lords
1831	24 April: Death of Kitty Wellington
1832	15 May: Wellington fails to form a government, Earl Grey recalled
	7 June: Great Reform Act
1834	Elected Chancellor of Oxford University
	15 November–9 December: Caretaker Prime Minister until return of Robert Peel
	9 December: Appointed Foreign Secretary
1835	7 April: Following the Tory defeat acts as Leader of Opposition in the Lords for next seven years
1841	Summer: Joins the Cabinet without office
1846	Spring: Encourages change of policy on the Corn Laws
1848	10 April: Chartist demonstration policed by Wellington
1850	Made Ranger of the Royal Parks
1851	1 May: Attends the Great Exhibition
1852	14 September: Death at Walmer Castle, Kent at the age of eighty-three.
	18 November: State funeral and burial in St Paul's Cathedral

Further reading

The classic, elegant and authoritative biography is by Elizabeth Longford; it is available in several editions: Elizabeth Longford, *Wellington*, part 1, *The Years of the Sword* (1969) and part 2, *Pillar of State* (1972) and *Wellington: a new biography*, abridged ed. (Sutton, 2001).

Christopher Hibbert's readable portrait of Wellington concentrates on the man, rather than the military leader: Christopher Hibbert, *Wellington: a personal history* (HarperCollins, 1997).

In contrast, Richard Holmes, *Wellington: the iron duke* (HarperCollins, 2003) finds Wellington 'easy to admire, harder, perhaps to like'.

Andrew Roberts, *Napoleon & Wellington* (Weidenfeld & Nicolson, 2001) provides a stimulating comparison with Wellington's great enemy.

The *Oxford Dictionary of National Biography* (2004) contains a substantial entry by the distinguished Wellington scholar, Norman Gash; second-hand bookshops may well proffer Philip Guedalla's addition to the 'great gallery of English prose': Philip Guedalla, *The Duke* (Hodder and Stoughton, 1931).

For an introduction to the military history of the period, Holmes provides the best starting point and convincingly captures the flavour of military life: Richard Holmes, *Redcoat: the British soldier in the age of horse and musket*

(HarperCollins, 2001).

Detailed histories of the campaigns are provided by the idiosyncratic but indispensable works of Jac Weller: Jac Weller, *Wellington in the Peninsula 1808-1814* (Greenhill, 1992), *Wellington at Waterloo* (Greenhill, 1992) and *Wellington in India* (Greenhill, 1993).

These should be read alongside the following: Ian Fletcher, *Galloping at Everything. The British Cavalry in the Peninsular War and at Waterloo, 1808-1815: a reappraisal* (Spellmount, 2000); Charles J. Esdaile, *The Peninsular War: a new history* (Allen Lane, 2002); Peter Hofschröer, *1815, the Waterloo Campaign: the German victory* (Greenhill, 1999), which provides an alternative view of Wellington's role at the battle of Waterloo and his relations with the Prussians.

A more intimate history of soldiering can be found in: Lt. Col. William Tomkinson, *Diary of a Cavalry Officer 1809-15 in the Peninsular and Waterloo Campaigns* (Spellmount, 1999).

On the more personal experience of those fighting on the French side: Alan Forrest, *Napoleon's Men. The soldiers of the Revolution and Empire* (Hambledon and London, 2002)

Wellington's political career is resurrected in the following: Norman Gash, *Wellington: studies in the military and political career of the first Duke of Wellington* (Manchester University Press, 1990); Peter Jupp,

British Politics on the Eve of Reform (Macmillan, 1998).

Candid reminiscences recorded by Wellington's friend the Earl of Stanhope give a sense of Wellington's character and underline the Victorian fascination with the man: *Earl of Stanhope, Notes and Conversations with the Duke of Wellington* (Prion, 1998).

Another side of nineteenth-century life can be found in Lesley Blanch (ed.), *Harriette Wilson's Memoirs* (Phoenix, 2003).

The Wellington Papers are held at Southampton University; the catalogues are available via the Internet and include the full text of many documents, together with an online exhibition: http://www.archives.lib.soton.ac.uk

Edited volumes of the bulk of Wellington's correspondence were produced in the nineteenth-century; most of the Duke's personal correspondence, however, was destroyed by him: Col J. Gurwood (ed.), *The Dispatches of Field Marshal the Duke of Wellington during his various campaigns in India, Denmark, Portugal, Spain, the Low Countries and France from 1799–1818*, 13 vols. (1834–1839); 2nd Duke of Wellington (ed.), *Despatches, Correspondence and Memoranda of Field Marshal Arthur, Duke of Wellington*, 8 vols (1867–1880); 2nd Duke of Wellington (ed.), *Supplementary Despatches and Memoranda of Field Marshal Arthur, Duke of Wellington KG*, 15 vols (1858–1872).

Index